The Box You Got

TRANSFORMING THE WORLD YOU LIVE IN

STEVE BIGARI

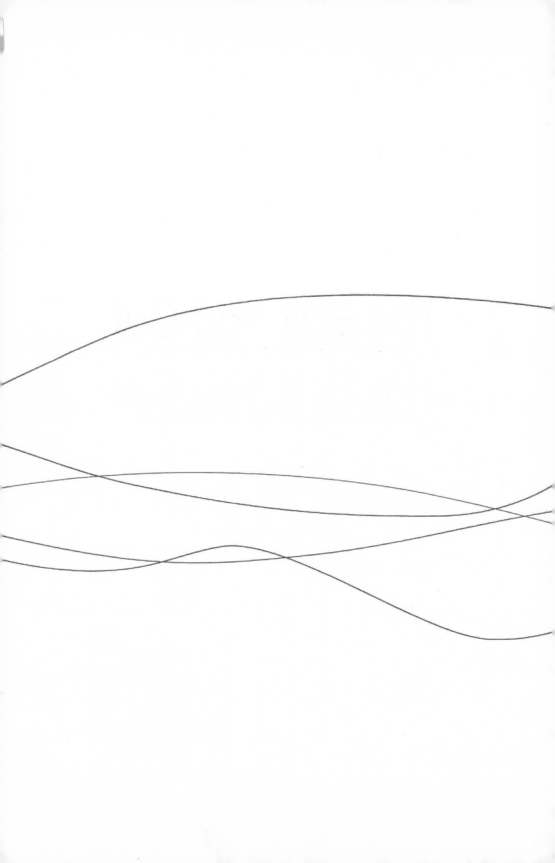

The Box You Got

TRANSFORMING THE WORLD YOU LIVE IN

INFECTIOUS EDITION

The Box You Got: Transforming
the World You Live In

Published by Elevation Press
1365 Garden of the Gods Road, Suite 120,
Colorado Springs, CO 80907

ISBN-13: 978-0-9791332-0-6
ISBN-10: 0-9791332-0-3

Cover design by Dina Snow, Azteca Design,
Colorado Springs, CO

Interior Design by Media Contractors, Inc.
www.mediacontractors.com

For further information go to:
www.theboxyougot.com
www.i3cms.com

Three Easy Steps to Transform
the World You Live in!

You are among the first readers to experience **The Box You Got.** *Help me launch the* **SEVEN DEGREES OF TRANSFORMATION BOOK TOUR** *by following the instructions below. Our mission is to transform the lives of 7,000 people by 7/7/07. You can start that process today by registering your book, reading it and then recycling it to another reader. Here's how:*

1. REGISTER!

Go to www.theboxyougot.com and register your copy of *The Box You Got.* By registering your book, you are eligible to receive coupons, discounts, and other prizes.

2. READ!

Sit down and read *The Box You Got* from cover to cover. It's packed with all my "Bigg Ideas" for how to unleash your passion.

3. RECYCLE!

Books don't belong on shelves. After you read *The Box You Got,* pass it along to a friend and tell him or her to start the process over again at step one. Sign your name below, and give it to someone else.

1. _____
   First Name Last Initial Email address City / State Email of person you
   gave it to

2. _____
   First Name Last Initial Email address City / State Email of person you
   gave it to

3. _____
   First Name Last Initial Email address City / State Email of person you
   gave it to

4. _____
   First Name Last Initial Email address City / State Email of person you
   gave it to

5. _____
   First Name Last Initial Email address City / State Email of person you
   gave it to

6. _____
   First Name Last Initial Email address City / State Email of person you
   gave it to

7. _____
   First Name Last Initial Email address City / State Email of person you
   gave it to

Reader #7, send your book back to me to receive a special gift!

Mail it to: Steve Bigari, 5825 Mark Dabling Boulevard, Colorado
Springs, CO 80919

More Praise for *The Box You Got*

The Box You Got is twenty years of leading-edge innovations that will help you find your dreams and set the course to get there. I'm giving it to every one of my own employees!

Keith Pascal
CEO
Torex Retail

When I first met Steve, I knew immediately that this was not your ordinary McDonald's owner/operator—this was a visionary who understood that his economic success was grist for the mill that helped produce success for others. I've had the privilege to watch Steve hone his skills to precision in the name of helping others. Reading *The Box You Got* won't make you into Steve, but it will help you come to grips with your inner abilities and your personal worth in helping others!

Arthur Polner
Certified Investment Management Analyst
Smith Barney

This book is a must-read! I could not put it down. Dinesh D'Souza asks in his terrific book, *What's So Great About America?* The answer: Steve Bigari.

Robert Balink
Co-Founder and Co-Editor
The Pound Ridge Rocket

Steve Bigari flat out "Gets It!" This is a must-read for anyone who has any thought or desire of getting ahead in life and/or business...and it should be required reading for everyone under 40. A quick read that will change your life!

COL Dick "The Skull" Johns, USA (Ret.)
Executive Director, Middle Atlantic Section
The PGA of America

For each of us who's ever thought about pursing a dream or making the world a better place, Steve Bigari, speaking from experience, says, "Why not?" "Here's how," and "Get up and do it!

Barbara Kazdan
Co-Director
U.S. Ashoka

A terrific read...at times it is irreverent humor but the message is totally relevant. Steve Bigari doesn't present theory but rather a pragmatic approach to changing the world one person at a time.

Roland DeRenzo
President
Handprints Early Education Centers Inc.

A practical, delightful story guaranteed to awaken the stuff of effective servant leadership in anyone, top executive or burger flipper! Jesus, the creative and compassionate Word of God, continues to become flesh in hearts open to imagination and vision, passion and persistence! Thank you, Steve Bigari!

The Rev. Paul F. Wicker
Pastor and Regional Vicar
Holy Apostles Episcopal Catholic Churrch
Colorado Springs

This book is dedicated to the 39 million hard-working people in America who, among other things, cook our food, clean our hotel rooms and care for our children. Your service and dedication inspire me! Thank you for all you do and always remember you *can* achieve the desires of your heart.

People tell me all the time, "Steve, you really think outside the box!" That's crap. I love the box! You can do a lot with a box. It doesn't matter if it's big or small, fat or thin. It can be an old box or a new box. I take all sorts of boxes and make new things out of them. It's not about thinking outside the box. That's what most people think because it's the conventional wisdom. I'll tell you: It's about what you do with the box you got.

Do what you can,
with what you have,
where you are.

Theodore Roosevelt

Contents

Acknowledgements

There are so many people who have shaped my thoughts and character. It's as if I am a quilt composed of a small part of each of them. I would like to start where the book ends by thanking Matt, Moira, Larry and Devlin from The Elevation Group. Larry and Devlin provide an atmosphere of excellence that is viral. Matt made me sound 50 percent smarter than I actually am, and Moira scrubbed the manuscript over and over. These two have become heroes to me because they have a passion for orphaned kids. I expect the three of us and our families will head to China when our kids are old enough to help a couple more orphans!

A special thanks to the social entrepreneurs who inspired me to leave the safety and security of a profitable business to try to change the world. To Barbara, Trabian and the team at Ashoka (ashoka.org), this epiphany began with you! To the Anschutz, El Pomar, Daniels and Coors Foundations, I offer my sincerest thanks for seeing my vision when others didn't believe. To Vanessa, Kim, Cheryl and the New Profit (newprofit.org) team: I have already learned so much from you. Thanks for dragging me to Mohunk!

My partners with whom I have labored side-by-side over the years at McDonalds's, America's Family (amfol.com), Biggs and the rest. Your service to others goes largely unrecognized, but I am forever inspired by each of you. Your tenacity and grit in the face of seemingly insurmountable odds is incredible. You face the most difficult situations with resolve, grace and humor. I am especially mindful of the single moms who love their kids enough to claw their way out of one jam after another. I will not rest until we can offer you opportunities that are as big as your dreams.

My teammates in business, at West Point and at Brown, and those from my high school football days, have written lessons on my heart and instilled resolve in my soul. Thanks to you, I don't know how to quit! During my journey, I met a man who is not mentioned in the rest of this book: John Dodson. He started as one of my professors at West Point. A soldier, entrepreneur, brother and friend of the highest order, I could have filled the pages of this book with stories of his life. He wouldn't want it that way. John was the catalyst for most everything that has transpired in my life up to now.

Finally, in this world there is nothing more important to me than my family. My beautiful wife, Brenda, is the best mom to our kids and partner a man could ever have. My precious children - Sara, Cali, Anna, Zachary and Matthew - are the air that fills my lungs. I don't deserve any of them, but thanks to my God, I get so much more than I deserve. The fact that He could love me is completely inexplicable. I am simply overcome with joy at what He does for me every day!

Introduction

I believe that everybody is a leader. The top exec, the carpool mom, the freshman biology student, the McDonald's burger-flipper—they're all leaders. You are too.

Conventional wisdom tells us that leaders are by nature charismatic and influential, and the word "leader" conjures up images of presidents and power-brokers. True, but if you study the world's greatest leaders you'll find much more to the picture. Really, they're people just like you. So I'm telling you: Throw out the idealized notion of leadership. We're all leaders.

BIGG IDEA: WE ARE ALL LEADERS.

If you don't think of yourself as a leader, don't fear. It just means you've never gotten in touch with your deepest passions. To steal an idea from John Maxwell, a leader is one who exerts influence over another in some way. Leadership is, fundamentally, about influence. You can be a leader in your family, your church or your business. Maybe you're a leader to your dog. Everyone has influence—and everyone has passion. It is the successful combination of the two that creates powerful leaders. The world's greatest leaders are passionate about something. It could be a product, an idea or a person—but the common denominator of transformative leadership is passion.

Throughout the book, I'll refer back to the concept of passionate or transformative leadership and illustrate it with philosophies that I call "BIGG IDEAS." This kind of leadership is for people who are willing to get in touch with their deepest passions and unleash them. It takes risk because it challenges conventional wisdom. It cuts against the grain.

I've been very successful by the world's standards. And that type of success comes with stereotypes. It's amazing what people think they know about me before I've even met them. But I'm just a guy. I say things that get me into trouble. I make bad business decisions. I yell when I should listen. I live with one of my two feet in my mouth most of the time. I have quirks—like trying to drink five liters of water each day. Oh, and I use the same Aquafina water bottle for about a week at a time. This drives my chief operating officer crazy. He thinks I'm the cheapest millionaire on the planet. I'm probably not, but in spite of my humanity, I've had great success. I believe you can too, and I want to help you achieve it. So I've written this book with you in mind.

You Are Holding a Cookbook

That's right: leadership is a lot like cooking. Great leaders have the cookbook, understand the concepts and know what they're supposed to do with them. But the most important ingredient is the passion that lies within them. Call it the flame. The burner. The convection oven. If this book does nothing else, I want it to unleash the passion for whatever you have in your life, so you can apply these principles and get the most out of them. Lots of people can learn how to cook, but very few people are chefs. In my 18 years as a McDonald's guy, I learned how to cook things. (It's more a food factory than a restaurant.) Still, every once in a while I'll take a stab at lasagna or a chocolate cake. Now, because of my "factory" background at McDonalds, I follow recipes to the letter. Not so for my friend, Matt Van Auken. He is an accomplished chef who takes an entirely different approach to food. Matt doesn't use recipes. For him, the recipe is just a guideline or suggestion. He looks at the ingredients and substitutes other things that he thinks will taste better. I can't even imagine doing that because I wouldn't know where to look or what to substitute. I don't even know the difference between baking soda and baking powder. That's why I stick to the recipe.

I'm no chef—my test kitchen is the business world. What you will find in this book are a number of practical principles or "ingredients" that have transformed my life and the lives of many of my employees. The thing about ingredients is that you don't have to combine them in exactly the same way to create something that tastes very good. This book will show you the ingredients, demonstrate how they interact and teach you how to combine them in your own life for the optimal outcome. You are writing your own leadership recipe, and you can deviate from these suggestions and change whatever you want. You might find yourself gravitating toward particular chapters and not others. That's because none of us has the same combination of talents and passions. But you must take the first step and decide what you want to create. Like Matt, you need to take these suggestions and come up with your own recipe. Each of the ingredients is something you can apply to your life right now, wherever you are. I can help you find your passion, and that passion will determine how the ingredients are put together, and what the results look like.

I really am just a guy who used to flip burgers at McDonald's, and now I'm living my dream to transform the lives of 39 million hard-working Americans by giving them access to services and relationships to build better lives. Isn't it great that we live in a country where I can sell profitable restaurant franchises in order to help others? Maybe this impresses you. (If it does, tell a friend so I can sell more books.) More than that, I hope it inspires you to get up, find your gift and get to work living your dream. Maybe you have this thing pulling at your heart that you can't describe, but you know there's something to it. By reading this, you're taking an important step in the right direction. This book ain't Shakespeare. It's just Steve Bigari. Let's get started!

P.S. A word of caution: There are no hard and fast rules or recipes in this book, just concepts. Steal them, try them, change them and keep what works for you. When you're finished, send me an e-mail (steve@i3cms.com) and let me know how they turned out for you.

Chapter 1

The Action Principle –
Gaining Momentum

He who would move the world
must first move himself.

Socrates

I'm going to tell you some great stories that illustrate
fundamental principles of passionate leadership. Those concepts,
and everything else in this book, revolve around what I call the
Action Principle. For any of this to work, you must get this. The
next **BIGG IDEA** is simple, and it goes like this:

GET UP OFF YOUR ASS
AND DO SOMETHING.

Print that out and put it in your office—right over your desk.
Heck, print one out and put it in your boss' office!

Deep down in your soul somewhere is a little pilot
light. Now, pilot lights don't do much. They just make it easier
to light up the grill when you're ready to turn on the fuel source.
Without the propane tank, the pilot light is pretty useless. You
can't cook a steak over a pilot light.

When I hear people whining about their lives, I
notice most of them are pretty talented—some are downright
brilliant—and many of them are sitting on their asses doing
nothing but complaining. Let's face it: we all do it from time

to time. Over the last 20 years, I've come to realize that most people don't see themselves the way others do. You probably have some great friends, family members, and co-workers who fit this description—talented people who don't have a clue how gifted they are. They go on about their confusion, lack of direction and inner turmoil. Maybe this even describes ... you.

Frankly, there's no place in my life for this type of thinking. We've all got gifts, and unless you get up off your ass, you can't do much with them. So ask yourself, "Am I sitting around?" If so, it may be because you're afraid.

Understanding Fear

Any motivational speaker worth his fees will tell you that fear is the dominant emotion in all human behavior. Fear, more than anything else, drives our behaviors. Unfortunately, being afraid does not get us very far and often prevents us from seeing who we really are.

There's an old Disney cartoon called "Lambert the Sheepish Lion." The basic story is that a lion cub somehow ends up abandoned in a herd of sheep. Raised by the sheep, Lambert thinks of himself as one of them. So when the wolves come around, Lambert cowers in fear as they terrorize the herd. The lion thinks he's a lamb! For most of the cartoon, he's copying what the other sheep are doing, which consists of a lot of bleating and running around. In the climax, Lambert's "mother" is cornered by one of the snarling wolves and bleats out to her son, "Lambert! Lambert!" Finally, it clicks, and the lion in Lambert comes blasting out. He lets out a deafening roar, setting the wolves running for their lives.

You see, Lambert was afraid of the wolves for no good reason. In life, this happens to the best of us. What I believe

Lambert is teaching us here is that in order to conquer our fears, we have to understand and embrace our true nature. When we are afraid of things that cannot hurt us, we often cower in life's corners—just like Lambert. If you're afraid, you can't get up and do much of anything. So how do you get rid of the fear?

In my experience, the best way out of fear-based thinking is to replace it with an action-driven lifestyle. Fear is stationary, inertia, drag. Action is fear's antidote, because in most cases, we are afraid of trying something new. Whether it's trying broccoli or baking a cherry pie, we are afraid that if we change our behavior we may have to experience something unpleasant, maybe even fail. This is why the Action Principle is key. By getting up and doing something, you are taking your first steps against fear. As an illustration, consider the story of Joe Johnson, a guy who took the first steps and is now out there living his dream.

Case Study: Joe Johnson

Joe was born in Okinawa, an island that is now part of Japan, in 1969. His father was an Airborne Ranger fighting in Vietnam and stationed in Okinawa, where he met his Japanese wife-to-be. They married in Japan, and soon afterwards Joe was born. After his father's tour in Vietnam was complete, the Johnsons relocated to Fort Carson in Colorado Springs, where Joe's younger brother and sister were born. Joe's dad continued in the military, while his mother stayed home raising the kids. In the late 1970s, Joe's father retired from active duty and took a civil service job in Saudi Arabia. Not long after, while overseas, Joe's dad had divorce papers delivered to his wife. Joe recalls standing in the garage, watching as a strange man approached the house and gave his mother a letter. Joe said, "From that day on, everything was different."

Relying on her own strong sense of survival and her friends in the Japanese community of Colorado Springs, Joe's mom began raising her three children alone. Following her example, Joe took jobs while he was in high school to contribute to the family budget, while juggling his own desires to do well in school, play sports, and enjoy a life of his own. But he knew his role as a brother and "father" to his younger siblings had to come first. He graduated from high school third in his class and was convinced that college was his next right move.

After high school, Joe and two of his buddies moved to Arizona. He wanted to start work on his associate's degree. While there, Joe picked up an entry-level job as a crew person at one of the local McDonald's restaurants. He chose McDonald's because he wanted to save money on food. During this time, Joe went to school from 8:00 am to 4:00 pm, returned home, changed, and then worked an eight-hour shift at McDonald's. By the time he had gotten his degree, Joe was swing manager— managing an entire shift of employees for the restaurant owner. Joe never thought he'd make a career out of McDonald's, but this college job set up the next twenty years of his life.

After college, Joe decided to move home to help his family. Just after he returned home, tragedy hit their family again. While riding with his mother, Joe's younger brother suffered a stroke. (I've never heard of a 15-year-old kid having a stroke, but that's exactly what happened.) This was the era before cell phones, so Joe's mother got out of the car, but she couldn't get anyone to stop and help her. Finally, she ran about a mile before finding a phone to call 911. By the time the paramedics got to Joe's brother, he had suffered significant brain damage. After about a week on life support, Joe and his mother made the decision to "pull the plug" just a few weeks before the brother's 16th birthday. I can only imagine the enormity of this decision. I think of Joe standing by his brother's bedside, confronting a decision that is supposed to come from a father— but instead falls to a son, a brother. This takes incredible guts, love and commitment. Sure, Joe probably thought, "Why is this happening to me?" But he never let that cripple him. He knew what needed to be done, and he did it with honor.

While grieving the loss of his brother, Joe knew he needed a good job. He wasn't sure what he wanted to do. Instead of waiting around to figure it out, he applied to work at one of the McDonald's restaurants I managed. At the time I wasn't a franchisee, but I managed 13 restaurants here in Colorado Springs. So Joe came in for an interview and laid out all his nice paperwork. He had a resume, some certifications, a bunch of references and a letter of recommendation from the other McDonald's restaurant. I could tell that this was a guy who would give his job everything—every day of his life. But I kept telling him, "Well, let's see what you can do." I was actually excited to hire him because we had some problems in the stores that I wanted to see if he could fix for me.

I put Joe in the toughest position I could find, as a swing manager for a store that had a load of problems— absenteeism, turnover, lack of teamwork, disarray, theft—the works. Joe describes that situation as going into a third-world country compared to anything he had encountered in Arizona. Over the next few years, I put Joe into even more challenging situations, and in each one he'd clean up the problem and move on. I don't know if he felt favored or abused; maybe both. Over the next several years, Joe became my right-hand guy. When I became a franchisee, I brought Joe with me, and he worked his way up to director of operations over all 12 of my McDonald's stores. He helped grow the business and in the process made McDonald's history. Our stores pioneered the "Made for You" food production system. Together, we helped reinvent how McDonald's prepares and serves food. Somewhere along the way, Joe developed a dream.

I worked with Joe to help him purchase his own McDonald's restaurant. I knew that I was going to sell the stores, and Joe already owned a portion of one of the new restaurants we had opened together. We developed the strategy and the financing for him to own the store outright as a McDonald's franchisee. We finalized the sale in June 2006, and I can't wait to see where Joe will take that store, and his career, in the future.

What Does It Mean to You?

You may be wondering how Joe's story applies to you. In the time he worked for me, Joe and I had many meetings to help him define his dream and come up with a strategy to achieve it. The following is a little system, very similar to what I used with Joe, that you can use to define your dreams, get beyond your fears and start moving forward in your life. It's a four-step process: Discern your dream, refine it, make your plan and then execute it.

Step 1: DISCERN
What Is Your Dream?

Do you know? You might say, like Joe did, "I think I want to own a restaurant one day." That's good—that's a dream. Perhaps you'd like to run a marathon or go skydiving. Those are good, too. Personal dreams can move you forward and spill over into other areas of your life. Even though I've accomplished some things, I keep dreaming. Today, my dream is to

**Help 39 million hard-working Americans
who are trapped in poverty connect to the resources
that will improve their lives and enable them to
achieve the highest level of prosperity.**

Like most people, I had no idea what this would entail when I came up with it. But I started to move. When you do that, dreams have consequences, big ones. Now it's your turn. To define your dream, fill in the rest of these sentences:

Before I die, I'd really like to...

I know I'm great at...

My pulse gets going when I...

Now that you've written those down, get to the bottom of your dream using what I call "The Whys" Drill. It works like this:

I want to spend my life helping 39 million hard-working Americans who are trapped in poverty connect to the resources that will improve their lives and enable them to achieve the highest level of prosperity.

WHY?

Because that was me growing up. I came from a working-class family in Wisconsin, and I want to use all of my business experience and influence to really make a difference.

WHY?

It's painful to me. When you own 12 McDonald's stores, you work with a lot of people who can't make ends meet. For some, an entry-level job is the only one they can get. And it's painful for me to watch families struggle through situations like this.

7

WHY?

Because I believe that every person who is able to work should have access to the same opportunities I have. For many low-wage earners, doors like "health care," "child care," "education," "home ownership," "transportation," and "computer skills" are closed and locked. I think they can and should be opened for almost everyone. In order for employers to provide these benefits, the cost of your goods and services would double or triple! You won't pay that. I had to find a collaborative solution.

WHY?

I've found that opening those doors isn't that hard, but does take resources. I have those resources. I have a lot of expertise about what works and what doesn't in helping families. I know where to get them connected. Since I have these skills, I want to use them.

WHY?

At the end of the day, that's just what I feel I was put here on earth to do. Whether it's helping a single mom get a car or sending a young kid back to school, it brings me the most overwhelming sense of completion and fulfillment I have ever experienced in life. Ultimately, that confirms I am in the right place.

If you're reading carefully, you'll see that my dream is all mapped out. It draws on my childhood, taps into my sense of fairness and wanting to help others, draws on my business experience and skills, and puts me in a place of fulfillment. Every dream should do this. If yours doesn't, start over. Sometimes when you complete this process, you find that your original dream is not really the root of your motivation. You may start out thinking that you want to be an author, when really you want to become a book agent! Follow all the rabbit trails that the "Whys" take you down. Explore them, and then dispense with the ones that aren't part of your true dream. Eventually, you'll hit the vein, and it will take you all the way down to your truest dreams. It's like finding gold. Often you'll discover that your dream is not really about what you thought it was. Always seek the deeper passion.

There's no magic number of "whys." The point is to keep asking "Why?" until you get to the very bottom—then, you can really build your strategy for accomplishing your dream.

Step 2: REFINE
Make a List of Pros and Cons

I like to make this step really simple, as in: Fit it on a 3x5 card. One of the problems of technology is the nearly unlimited space it gives us. If you sit down to write on a computer, you could write something of infinite length. This exercise requires more boundaries. Either way, you need to write your pros and cons. Put a + on one side, a – on the other, and a line separating them into two columns. You might think, "This is some great advice Bigari's giving me!" It might seem simple, but it's an excellent exercise. If you are familiar with strategic planning, then you've probably heard of a "SWOT Analysis" (strengths, weaknesses, opportunities and threats). This is the point where you take your dream and make an inventory of all the strengths, weaknesses, opportunities, and threats you have available to you. Start to "laundry list" everything you can think of for these categories. Keep this in mind:

9

All Pros and Cons Are Not Equal!

Some people mistake this for an exercise in which you list concerns of equal weight, and the longer list wins out in every case. That's a huge mistake. Your pros and cons are often of unequal weight. Some may be enormous in their implications—like having to quit your job and have your spouse go back to work. Others may be trivial or undefined, like the sense of risk that you assume in order to take on a new venture. You've got to weigh them appropriately and know which are the most important factors.

When I was deciding to whether to stay in the Army, I had a huge list of pros and only one con. That one negative was that with military benefits, my daughter Sara wouldn't get the best medical care for her host of birth defects. That outweighed every positive thing, and the decision was easy. Ironically, this decision led me to the Ronald McDonald house, which led me to McDonald's franchise owner Brent Cameron and my career as a McDonald's franchisee.

Last thing: Remember that you need to inventory your internal strengths and weaknesses along with the external threats and opportunities that are affecting your environment. Those external factors may influence you to wait for a year or two because, for example, the market for your innovative idea is not right at the moment. This factor influenced my own decision. The fast-food market was at a high when I sold my stores. If it hadn't been, I would have had to ride the trend until the market improved. Be sure to separate your internal and external factors and, again, weigh them appropriately.

Step 3: PLAN
Developing Your Options

Once you've passed through step 2, it's likely that you've accepted whatever inherent risks and rewards your dream holds, and you're ready to move forward. Now you need to map the different options to get to your destination. Let me be extremely clear here:

There Are Many Paths to Achieving Your Dream.

This is something people often miss. You've got options. Doing nothing is always an option, although rarely a good one. If your dream is to buy a restaurant one day, you could:

- Do nothing
- Buy a franchise
- Go to work for a franchisee
- Take a job with a franchised company
- Become an owner/operator (which can be a different model from franchising)
- Build a restaurant from scratch
- Go to work with a restaurateur and buy his or her restaurant over time.

You've got options—and there are tons more. Your next job is to list your options and start pursuing the ones that make the most sense given your pros and cons assessment in step 2. What does that look like in practice?

First, you need to consider who else is needed in the mix to make the option viable. Take Joe Johnson: The only way he could buy a McDonald's was through the relationship he had with me. He needed my pull with McDonald's and access to the

11

capital I could leverage for him. So I had to buy into his dream. Very rarely can you achieve a dream on your own. You've got to identify whom this affects before you start down a path.

Second, you can jump between options. In the restaurant example, maybe you want to become a franchisee because that market has the best opportunities for growth, but really, you're just parking your money there to let it grow. You sell at a high, and then jump over to a different restaurant model—casual dining, let's say. This is why it is worthwhile to map out a couple of good options that will bring you to your preferred future, your vision.

Third, and most importantly, you can and should seek the help of experts, mentors and other trusted advisors when you are making your plans. Make sure you know the tax implications for your investment decisions and changes to income. Talk to your financial planner to determine how this impacts the household budget or the college saving plan. Lots of people don't plan this far ahead and then they are stuck. When you gather advice and counsel, you are really refining your options even further. Get good information and advice, and put it to good use.

Step 4: EXECUTE

Guess what? We're back to the Action Principle. It's time to get up off your ass and put your plan into action. Good luck!

Moving Beyond Fear

This chapter is designed to move you beyond fears that will keep you from achieving your dream. At some point in his life, Joe Johnson made a decision to leave his fears behind. This wasn't easy, but here were some of the dynamics:

1)   Joe found his inspiration.

Think about the things in this world that matter most to you. These are probably the people and projects that will best motivate you. Even in Joe's case study you can see the things that motivated Joe—survival, work ethic, serving others. Owning a McDonald's restaurant helped Joe apply those motivations.

2)   Joe instigated change in his life.

Joe is making a difference because he decided to act. At times we decide to act out of sheer survival. Our reflexes take over and we jump into action. But like a deer in the headlights, sometimes we are so mesmerized—and paralyzed—by oncoming disaster that we allow it to run us over. Joe could have let life run him over. In fact, Joe told me that his mom's friends in Japan used to tell her to give up and come back home. But she refused to let life run her over. Listen: Even a bad decision is better than no decision at all because you're taking a step, getting forward momentum. You've got to act decisively.

3)   Joe constantly leveraged his skills.

Like a good leader, Joe took his modest success as a McDonald's crew person and leveraged that into better positions within the company. Eventually he even leveraged me out of my job so he could own the restaurant! Joe's story is uncommon in most companies, but an amazing number of McDonald's employees have become owners—including me. How do you leverage yourself? You've got to get in touch with your unique set of strengths and gifts. There are things you do better than others. In some roles, you might be the only person who can get the job done. Spend time on these things. This gives you the highest amount of leverage.

Whether you are a cartoon lion, a McDonald's crew person, middle manager, parent, student or stay-at-home mom, these are three hugely important principles for your life:

Inspiration – The Power of "Why Not?"

Instigation – The Power of Action

Innovation – The Power of Interactive Relationships

Each of these principles holds an invaluable key to unlocking your potential and your dreams for the future. The next three chapters are devoted to exploring these ideas and giving you the skills and knowledge to put them to good use.

Chapter 2

~~~~~

Inspiration – The
Power of "Why Not?"

Some men see things as
they are and say, "Why?"

I dream things that never
were and say, "Why not?"

George Bernard Shaw

A recent Visa credit card ad features a series of business meetings where all of the participants are wondering what the others are doing. As the camera moves between their various offices, it's obvious that each company is trying to copy the other. They want to steal each other's ideas! The commercial ends with "Business takes inspiration, business takes Visa."[1] I like this little commercial because it gets at the heart of what inspiration really is, and it isn't mimicking your competitors. Nonetheless, it is true that inspiration is difficult to come by and sustain. Often we're left with nothing more inspiring than, "Let's find out what the other guys are inspired by and copy that." I happen to think that's a poor approach. Inspiration is about how you see the world. There are a whole bunch of people—like the ones in the commercial—who are copying their neighbors. They're practicing the old conventional wisdom of "fake it till you make it." It doesn't work. People who find true inspiration are able to see the world from different, and sometimes really bizarre, angles. I'm going to take you back in time to my teenage years, when football was my life. As you get to know my younger self, you'll see how many of the seeds of inspiration were planted.

Hard-Knock Inspiration

When I was in high school, I learned something about inspiration on the football field. My high school coach, Bill Quinn, was a mountain of a man. He commanded the respect of players, fans, refs and school administrators. Because I was so invested in football, Quinn's coaching left a big impression on my life. Sometimes that coaching left literal impressions. In my senior year, I was the captain of the football team and played every minute of every game. Whether it was kickoff, punt return, offense, defense or the coin toss, I was on the field. One day, we were playing a non-conference game against a big private school called Madison Edgewood. We were supposed to get crushed, and that was all we heard about during the weeks leading up to the game.

Once we got on the field, we were doing the crushing. Our team ran circles around those prep school boys, holding them to only 100 yards of total offense. They did get a couple of good plays. One was a little swing pass where the quarterback floated the ball over my hands to the halfback for a 15-yard gain. Five plays later, I saw them line up for the same play. This time, I nailed the halfback while he was trying to catch the ball, which bounced off his helmet. After the tackle, the guy was looking out the ear hole of his helmet, wondering if he was still in the same zip code. I got up, leaned over and taunted him through his ear hole while he stumbled to get up and fix his gear.

As I went to line up, Coach Quinn signaled for me to come off the field. I couldn't believe it! After that great play, Quinn was calling me out of the game. I jogged over to him and said, "Yeah, Coach?" I'll never forget the inspiration he imparted. In front of 20,000 fans, Quinn set me on my tail. Then he leaned over to me and said, "Anything you got to say, you say it between the whistles! You understand me?"

"Yes, Coach," I stammered back.

"Then get your ass back in there," Quinn barked.

On that day, Coach Quinn left me with an important set of lessons I've never forgotten. First, do your talking on the playing field – with your actions, not your commentary. Second, don't let your team get away with behavior that's unacceptable. Moral and ethical standards—including those for sportsmanlike behavior—are not negotiable! And third, know when to make a dramatic statement that reinforces your expectations.

The last time I saw Coach Quinn was at my 20-year high school reunion. He wasn't the vigorous young man I remembered from high school. Multiple sclerosis had atrophied his body and confined him to a wheelchair. Quinn's wife was at the reunion, and you could tell that everyone was uneasy. We players all idolized Quinn. Yet the man who sat before us bore little physical resemblance to the Coach Quinn of our memories.

I noticed that no one had gone over to talk to Quinn or his wife, Cora. So I sat down with them, placed one hand on each of their shoulders and retold the story about the Madison Edgewood game and all the other things Coach used to make me do that helped me to become the man I am today. Halfway through the story, we all started bawling. Others started to notice what was happening and began to form a line. A parade of men sat down with Cora and Quinn to say, "Let me tell you what you meant to me when you were my football coach." This went on for the whole night: Hugs. Stories. Tears.

Don't get me wrong I didn't enjoy being humiliated by my coach in front of 20,000 people. I hated many of the things he made us do, because most of the time it pushed me so hard I thought I was literally going to throw up – or die! Now, when I look back on Coach Quinn, I realize that he knew how to build strong men. He had a vision for us that extended far beyond the football field and our own expectations. The mighty Quinn wanted us to become men of integrity, talent and vision. I am part of the Bill Quinn legacy, as are dozens of other men who had the privilege of playing on one of his teams.

Bill Quinn inspired me to become a better man. Playing on his team meant everything to me. I didn't know it at the time, but that was part of Quinn's strategy. He knew that football was just a tool – something that gets high school boys (and I think men of all ages) pretty fired up. But football isn't the point of the story. It's about how Quinn inspired us to practice harder, play better and become better men. I want to show you how you can get inspiration like that in your life.

The Inspiration You Get

There are two types of inspiration: the kind you get and the kind you give. When you get inspired, it's usually very powerful and personal. According to legend, Paul McCartney woke up one morning with the melody and lyrics for "Yesterday" running through his head. Now, "Yesterday" is not just a great song, it's one of the most popular songs in the history of modern music! *The Guinness Book of World Records* says there are 2,500 known "covers" of "Yesterday" and over seven million performances of the song in the twentieth century.[2] One of the most popular songs of the last 50 years came to Paul McCartney in a dream.

For me, this is the gold standard of inspiration. The problem with stories like this is we think inspiration *must* come to us in dreams and visions. It can, but you can find your inspiration in just about anything: a pencil, a flower, a pitcher of lemonade or a traffic jam. I already told you that I found inspiration in Bill Quinn. You might have the McCartney dream, but I'd rather you have the Coach Quinn experience.

The Inspiration You Give

Let's also talk about the kind of inspiration you can give away. This has lots of parallels to the concept of "vision" and we'll come back to explore that in Chapter 5. John F. Kennedy laid out one of the most ambitious national visions in our country's history when he announced in 1961 that the US would put a man on the moon before the end of that decade.[3] Why did Kennedy make this announcement? In hindsight, it was a monumental vision. However, his inspiration was completely practical.

Kennedy's space initiative was about beating the Russians. The Russians had already beaten us to space, and Kennedy knew that if we lost the race to put a man on the moon, the US would lose a technological advantage for at least a generation. Instead, he came up with a vision to put Americans on the moon first, and in the process he catapulted American science and technology forward—leaving the Russians far behind in that race. This, I believe, sets the stage for President Reagan's strategy of spending the Soviets to death.[4] That's a big, risky vision with a lot at stake. If Kennedy or Reagan had failed in their pursuits, they could have bankrupted the country, kicked off a worldwide depression or even destroyed the American way of life.

President Kennedy saw something that never was—a man on the moon. In 1962, that was science fiction, not public policy. That vision for "things that never were" inspired our nation's greatest scientists, engineers and thinkers to say, "Why not?" This is the kind of inspiration that you give away to others. If Kennedy had been unsuccessful at inspiring the scientists, the space initiative would have failed. Interestingly, this is not unlike initiatives of Presidents Bill Clinton and George W. Bush. Clinton tried to inspire the public with the idea of universal healthcare for all Americans. Bush attempted to overhaul our Social Security program by allowing workers to invest in private retirement accounts. In both cases, this inspiration did not extend past a tight circle of policy wonks and political pundits in Washington, DC. The ideas made good headlines for a few months, but people just didn't latch on to them.

The Power of "Why Not?"

Sometimes ideas come in dreams and visions like McCartney's. But a practical leader, even one with vision, can't rely on the unpredictable subconscious. If you are waiting around for your divine inspiration—it could be a while. Other inspiration comes from sheer practical considerations, like President Kennedy's space program. For the rest of us, I believe we're somewhere in the middle. We draw our inspiration from things that are bigger than ourselves, people like Coach Bill Quinn. If you break it down, most of our inspirations are a fusion of practical realities and a dream for a better future. Bill Quinn embodied these principles. As a football coach, he had some practical realities: Win football games. Even back then, coaches got fired for losing records. He also knew he couldn't win football games without great players. He made us believe that our dream was winning games—again, the practical side. In truth, Quinn was much more concerned with our personal character as young men. There isn't anything our team wouldn't have done for him, and that is the truest inspiration I can imagine.

Getting to the Power of "Why Not?"

Out of inspiration come the seeds of innovation, which is why I believe that inspiration is about *how* you see the world. Again, conventional wisdom says that inspiration falls upon us like it did on McCartney. Those are good stories—but poor examples.

Cali, my second daughter, said to me once, "Why can't McDonald's have a better playground for kids?" In Chapter 11, you'll find out how we turned that question into a brand-new line of playgrounds for McDonald's. The point is, Cali was able to see things from a different angle. In this case, it was through the eyes and experiences of a child.

Putting Inspiration to Work in Your Life

BIGG IDEA: ADOPT THE ATTITUDE OF "WHY NOT"?

Inspiration requires three things from you: openness, attention and perspective. They will not simply drop from the sky. Incorporating these action-driven characteristics into your life requires intentional work and discipline. In the next few pages, we'll explore what that means.

1) Openness: Embracing New Ideas

You need to constantly train your mind to look for new things and ask, "How could I improve that?" Most of my inspiration has come from the practice of cobbling together existing ideas into things no one ever dreamed of. In fact, all of my three patents are for unique combinations of existing technology. Most of us are opposed to new ways of thinking. For all the talk of change and change agents in business, we are drawn to the comfortable and the familiar. And we wonder why we aren't inspired! Here's an idea that may be new for you: *You probably don't know as much as you think you do.* Seriously, you really don't. If that's hard for you to hear, if you've got a problem with change and new ways of thinking, now's your chance to admit it. Then work to embrace new ideas—even if they seem dangerous, countercultural or childish at the outset. If you have the desire to cultivate an open mind, you can train your brain to look for new opportunities wherever you go. You'll be saying, "Why not?" And once you start looking, you'll find all sorts of things that you never saw before. Every new idea challenges the *status quo,* and by embracing the new and unfamiliar, you are refining your ability to see the world through new eyes.

2) Attention: Eyes Wide Open

You can train yourself to always be on the lookout for new opportunities. Sit up front in meetings. As you listen, imagine how this idea or concept fits into your life. When I head to the back of the room during a meeting break to the table with coffee and cookies, I'm not just thinking about the cookies. I love cookies, but I use them as bait because people let their guards down on breaks. Be on the lookout for these opportunities. In the workplace, this might be at a lunch meeting, in the bathroom or in a parking lot when someone is walking to his car. When people's internal barriers come down, you have the potential to get the most work done. People are naturally defensive and protective—especially in the workplace. When a person's guard is down, you are speaking to her on a more relaxed and comfortable footing. Most of your work is done! A lot of good businesspeople get their deals closed on the golf course. It's not always because they love golf; it's because communication can flow more freely. There is no agenda or expectation, which provides the perfect opportunity to get things done. Golf is a way that wealthy guys network with one another. If golf isn't your thing, you might approach your boss after the next staff meeting to ask an unexpected question. As guards go down, your ability to inspire others goes up. In these settings, you can get things accomplished that you never thought possible. At your next meeting, try using the cookie table to pitch someone on a new idea. (And let me know how it goes!)

3) Perspective: The "God's-Eye" View

When I think strategically, I imagine tearing the roof off my house, my business or even the world. Google Earth (www.earth.google.com) is one of my favorite inventions because it helps you see the world from this perspective. Download Google Earth, look at your house, business or community and see it for what it is: a living, breathing set of interactions and systems. You'll begin to understand why things happen—and only then can you influence them. The view from behind your desk is not enough to get you truly inspired. You've got to get out of the building and into orbit before you see how things connect and interact. Let's say you're walking down the hall and you overhear

23

two subordinates arguing about a trivial matter. Simply looking at the argument from "behind the desk" doesn't yield enough information for you to understand what's going on. The only way to really understand the dynamic is to look from different angles—above, behind, around and through. Then you can see that the argument is just a symptom of something much deeper that needs repair, like employee morale. When you develop the vision to see through everyday interaction and down to the systemic level of operation, you can become inspired to change and improve it. This is where inspiration ends, and instigation begins.

Chapter 3

Instigation – The Power of Intent

Suit the action to the word,
the word to the action.

William Shakespeare

Immediately following the hurricane Katrina disaster in August 2005, millions of Americans rallied to help the citizens of New Orleans. The storm revealed many things that are usually hidden from our view. Every night our televisions broadcast unbelievable stories of loss. Each morning the papers carried headlines of government mismanagement. With each passing day, it became harder to hide the fact that many of the people living in New Orleans were extremely poor Americans with very few resources. All of these revelations brought Americans together to help. As with most tragedies, Hollywood also responded with the standard celebrity telethons. These fundraisers are usually so tightly scripted that you barely recognize the famous people talking to you, because they are so out of character. Anyone who was watching on Sunday, September 2, 2005, was treated to a rare instance where someone went off-script.

Kanye West, a popular young black rapper, was paired with comedian Mike Myers. Here's their transcript in its entirety:

Myers: *The landscape of the city has changed dramatically, tragically and perhaps irreversibly. There is now over 25 feet of water where there was once city streets and thriving neighborhoods.*

West: *I hate the way they portray us in the media. You see a black family, it says, "They're looting." You see a white family, it says, "They're looking for food." And, you know, it's been five days [waiting for federal help] because most of the people are black. And even for me to complain about it, I would be a hypocrite because I've tried to turn away from the TV because it's too hard to watch. I've even been shopping before even giving a donation, so now I'm calling my business manager right now to see what is the biggest amount I can give, and just to imagine if I was down there, and those are my people down there. So anybody out there that wants to do anything that we can help—with the way America is set up to help the poor, the black people, the less well-off, as slow as possible. I mean, the Red Cross is doing everything they can. We already realize a lot of people that could help are at war right now, fighting another way—and they've given them permission to go down and shoot us!*

Myers: *And subtle, but in many ways even more profoundly devastating, is the lasting damage to the survivors' will to rebuild and remain in the area. The destruction of the spirit of the people of southern Louisiana and Mississippi may end up being the most tragic loss of all.*

West: *George Bush doesn't care about black people!*

Myers: *Please call...*[5]

At this point, the segment was cut off. Someone at NBC woke up and put a stop to West's tirade, but the damage had already been done. Some found it sad, others funny, and many thought it was way out of line. I disagree with his assertion. But guess what? West is an instigator. He wasn't afraid to speak his mind and provoke a response on an issue of importance to him.

26

Regardless of what you thought of West's comments, he changed the environment from "nice telethon with famous people" to "someone getting real about racial double standards in the media." I believe that in this country, the poor are invisible. Katrina, and perhaps comments like West's, helped us to see their situation with raw and brutal honesty.

I'm not using this example to prompt you to walk into your next salary negotiation and blast your boss with some outrageous statement. The point is to use instigation strategically as a way to create an environment for success.

I do this with my employees during performance reviews. Usually people are pretty intimidated because there's a lot a stake for them. That's not a great way to have a conversation, so I usually start by asking the employee a series of preparation questions. As I pretend to make notes in their personnel file, I ask in a serious tone, "Does 'dumb ass' have a hyphen?" Then, with equal gravity, I follow up with, "Does 'buffoon' have one 'f' or two?" These questions have nothing to do with employee performance, and no boss would ever really ask these questions. But because the employee thinks I'm going to ask a serious question, my stupid joke makes them laugh. At that point, I've created an environment for a successful review, one that's relaxed and open. Once you get someone laughing, he or she can usually talk more freely and feel more at ease. That's just one way you can be an instigator. Sometimes you have to dial it up like West did during the fundraiser. I had to do this once, and it cost me my job at the time.

The Patient Guy and the Right Guy

After I graduated from high school, I was accepted into Brown University to play football on an academic scholarship.

I never really fit in at Brown, and the following year I found myself playing football for another school that had recruited me: the US Military Academy at West Point. My initial idea was to go there for a summer, learn some cool Army stuff and hit the University of Wisconsin with a crew cut and some cool stories. I thought it would help me get dates. But that initial summer turned into four years and eventually a military career as an engineer who got really good at blowing stuff up.

While I was in the military, my oldest daughter, Sara, was born. To say that she was a walking medical dictionary would be an understatement. In fact, the first thing the doctor said to me after she was born was, "Don't get too attached." She suffered from a variety of birth defects and ailments that required specialized surgery at the Children's Hospital in Denver, Colorado. These difficult medical experiences have shaped her character in ways I never could have imagined. Her most recent surgery was a total skull reconstruction at age 18. You walk away from those experiences changed—and stronger. Today, Sara is in nursing school and is the most beautiful, vibrant, intelligent young woman on the planet. That's not just a proud dad talking; if you ever meet her, you'll know exactly what I mean.

After Sara was born, my family lived in the Ronald McDonald House, and through that experience, I joined the board of directors. I wanted to help out this great organization that focused on helping kids and families in times of great need. I wanted to give back a little of what they had given to us. By this time, I was on my way out of the military and looking for a good job. One of the other board members, Brent Cameron, owned ten McDonald's restaurants in Colorado Springs and offered me a position in his company. I realized for the first time that my education got me noticed; getting noticed got me a relationship with Brent; and that relationship turned into a job offer. I was full of myself, so I turned him down to go work for Johnson & Johnson (J&J) in New Jersey. Actually, I had seven offers from Fortune 100 companies. I couldn't see how Brent could offer me more than these great organizations. He looked me in the eye after I turned him down and said, "You think you're going to like it there. But you're going to find that you're just another stiff in a Brooks Brothers suit. You're going to hate it. I know. I was there. So when you get there, and you realize that I was right, understand that I'm a patient guy and you're the right guy. So call me."

I got to J&J and hated it from the start. It just wasn't me. I lied to myself for four months until one day when the production plant panty shield machine broke. (Didn't I mention that? The division of J&J I worked for manufactured feminine hygiene products. Yeah, I did a little time on the Stay-Free Maxi-Pad line.) Like many factories, J&J's operation was controlled by union labor, and there were books and books of rules about everything—but especially repairs to machinery. That day, we only had one mechanic when the machine broke and the union required two for safety purposes. Now, by the rules, I was supposed to watch a bunch of hard-working men and women sit around. I thought this was pretty stupid, so I loosened up my tie, rolled up my sleeves and helped the one mechanic make the repairs. Everybody clapped and cheered, and we all went back to work for the day. Next thing I knew, the union vice president filed a grievance against me for violating union rules. I took the grievance to the plant manager and handed it to him along with my letter of resignation.

His mouth dropped open, and he kept saying, "You could be a director of this company one day. You have great potential. You can't leave!"

"Yeah," I said, "I don't think the culture is right for me. You see, nobody cares about the product. Those people, who were cheering out there, they want to care about their jobs. They want to take pride in their work. But the rules don't let them, and I can't deal with rules like that."

I love the company—still do—but I couldn't work in a place where the rules were more important than the relationships. I got back on a plane and flew out to Colorado Springs to sit down with Brent Cameron again. As he had predicted, there was no way I was going to fit into the J&J culture. Fortunately, Brent really was a patient man.

I was determined to work for him, but only if he agreed that I could learn every person's job before I was a supervisor. Little did I know, the McDonald's culture requires everyone to work as a crew person before taking a management position. This was Brent's biggest concern about bringing me on board. He was worried that I thought I was a big shot who didn't want to get my hands dirty with real work. He knew I was coming from J&J with a salary he couldn't match, with a fancy title and a lot of wonderful benefits. But he made me the offer. "Can you work for this amount?" he said, and pushed a piece of paper my way. It was a big pay cut. I looked at Brent and said, "Yeah, I can accept the pay cut and everything else. But you have to promise me that you'll let me do all the jobs so I can learn the business from the bottom up." He leaned back with this big Cheshire cat grin and said, "I think that could be arranged."

In three weeks, I was scrubbing urinals and thinking, "He knew! He knew that this would happen!" Brent sent me up to another operator's restaurant, a guy named Leroy Schmidt, so I could learn the business without making mistakes in front of my subordinates. He thought it was really important that I not screw up in front of the team that I'd soon be leading. Leroy was a great person, businessman and McDonald's operator, so I was taught well.

BIGG IDEA: USE THOUGHTFUL INSTIGATION TO MAKE YOUR POINT.

Being an Instigator

In this story, Brent and I were both instigators. I had to challenge the J&J culture—it's in my blood. And Brent was a really smart man who had been down the roads I thought I wanted to travel. He tried to instigate—but I wouldn't listen. Like inspiration, instigation is also divided into the type you get and the type you give. In life, you need to become an instigator, but you also need to know who the instigators are in *your* life. Listen to them, even if they are wrong. They may just cause you to get up off your ass...and action is where it all starts.

The Process of Instigation

Instigation is not just about stirring the pot because it's a fun thing to do. It's a very specialized and controlled process that you have to take time to master. Here are the key things you need to remember:

1)   Choose your battles.

You should consider instigation only when it's important and the stakes are high. Resist the temptation to stick your nose into everything, because there is a fine line between being an instigator and being a pest! Once you cross that line, it's impossible to regain your credibility.

31

2) Make a powerful statement.

Once you've selected the battle, study the opportunities available to you. You need to decide how, when and where to "drop a bomb" on the situation. Most importantly, you need to be sure your action is strong enough to provoke response. Too little and it'll be overlooked. Too much, and people might truly get hurt. If you are typically quiet and mild-mannered, a good, well-timed outburst could be ideal.

3) Offer clear guidance post-instigation guidance.

Once you start the instigation, it is important to have a detailed plan about how to get the result you're looking for. Your tirade could cause chaos. The problem with Kanye West's outburst is that he had no power to affect what came next. He couldn't fix the racial double standard in the media, so his work was only half done. As an instigator, you need to make sure you have the influence to fix the problem you've identified. Don't make the mistake of picking a battle you cannot win. *Before* you start, make sure you have a clearly defined action plan and execute it promptly.

Case Study: Steve and the Drive-Thru

Back in 1992, I owned just one McDonald's restaurant in Colorado Springs. I started noticing that at around 1:00 pm each day, the store's drive-thru lane would get backed up. This was right around when the shifts changed, and every day there was a predictable slowdown. I was concerned that during the lunch timeframe, our operation was overwhelmed with inefficiency. I knew my people were properly trained to do their jobs well. The problem was a lack of focus. I brought this to the attention of the shift managers in one of our regular meetings,

32

reinforcing that we needed to improve our drive-thru transaction times during the lunchtime hours. Seventy-five percent of our business came by way of the drive-thru. What I needed to get across was that improving the drive-thru line was our store's number-one priority. Still, the problem persisted. The second time I addressed the issue, I raised my voice a little—hitting the same key points with my managers. Still, nothing changed. At this point, it was clear to me that I needed a dramatic statement to get the performance I wanted.

One of the keys to instigation is to make it appear spontaneous. The only way to really pull that off is by planning far in advance what you're going to do. Think about it: You don't really want to instigate when you're angry. There are too many variables that could get out of hand. Once the "fight-or-flight" instinct rises up within you, it's hard to think like a rational person. Don't instigate when you're angry—always plan ahead. Over the course of a week, I planned my instigation. In doing so, I kept three things in mind: 1) I needed everyone to understand the importance of the drive-thru, 2) I needed to use very few words and 3) I needed my message to pass like a virus throughout the restaurant.

Just before 1:00, I picked up my clipboard and walked over to the drive-thru line. I meticulously started taking notes on the length of the individual transactions. The drive-thru was backed up again. Suddenly, the restaurant exploded with activity. Crew people were running around trying to speed up the drive-thru once they saw me taking times. After about ten minutes of this, I walked up to the front counter of the store—right where all the customers pay for their food. I slammed the clipboard down on the countertop, bringing activity to a halt. Even the customers were looking at me wondering what in the world was happening. Then, I picked up a packet of McDonald's BBQ sauce and gently opened one corner. "I can't believe that I'm talking about the drive-thru to you people again!" I said in a very loud voice. Now, the sauce was in my right hand, slightly opened and ready for launch. "I'm sick and tired of this," I shouted, and then threw the BBQ sauce 30 feet where it splattered all over the back wall of my restaurant. The packet landed exactly where I wanted it—between the drive-thru cashier and the manager's office. "Now when I come back," I said, "you'd better have this figured out!" I "stormed" out of the restaurant, got into my car and started laughing as I took a drive around the block to "cool down."

I never had to talk about the drive-thru again to my employees again. To this day, people still talk about the day Steve Bigari snapped and threw BBQ sauce all over the store. It's an urban legend. I love it, because the whole situation was directly under my control, and for years this story has been passed down to new hires who quickly learn that Steve Bigari means what he says. It was all planned in advance so I would achieve my goals and not hurt anyone. It worked better than I ever could have expected.

As you think about using instigation in your own life, use this example as a tool for how you plan your "outburst." But remember, if you are known to shout, try the quiet approach. You have to make sure that whatever you do is so out of character that people stop and say, "He's really upset, and we've got to change this!"

The last piece of wisdom I'll share about instigation is the importance of importance. Maybe you didn't get that. Instigate only when it's important, when everyone needs to hear the same lesson and when the stakes are high. Good luck, and let me know if you need any help getting BBQ sauce stains off your walls.

Chapter 4

Innovation — The Power of
Interactive Relationships

*Think big about what you can achieve; think small about
how to achieve it. That's because you get things done through
individuals and small groups of individuals.*

General Bill Creech

People tell me all the time, "Steve, you really think outside the box!" That's crap. I love the box! You can do a lot with a box. It doesn't matter if it's big or small, fat or thin. It can be an old box or a new box. You start with what you have and make it better.

BIGG IDEA: IT'S WHAT YOU DO WITH THE BOX YOU GOT!

Even if one person is the prime instigator, innovation can't happen in a vacuum. You need to find the right people, with the right tools, who have a clear vision and long view when it comes to accomplishing your goal. You'll run into short-sighted people. But if you're sold on your vision, you will think, push, break through, climb over or go around anything—or anyone—standing in your way. As you work to accomplish your goals, always remember: You can never rationalize unethical conduct.

Why Not McPlastic?

About six months into my job managing McDonald's stores with Brent, I had the first of many opportunities to test the ideas of practical leadership—to be specific, innovation. At the time, I was managing one of Brent's stores, and my family showed up for dinner. I didn't have any money, so I couldn't buy food for the kids. At that time, McDonald's didn't take credit cards (it was 1990). Credit cards didn't fit with McDonald's promise of "fast" food. When I asked about it, I was told, "Credit cards will never work at McDonald's." The people who said this were not stupid; they just operated from a different paradigm than mine. I wanted to break down their paradigm—and figure out how I could buy my kids a Happy Meal with my credit card.

Over the course of a few months, I took some existing credit card authorization hardware and software and created an in-store machine that allowed customers to "create cash" with their credit cards. No one had ever used this combination, so my first two patents came from this little device. With it, I could pre-approve my credit card for $20.00, get a little receipt, stand in line for my food, order my food, and give the slip to the McDonald's crew person. The cashier would write in the appropriate amount, and at the end of the day reconcile the amount that I authorized with the exact amount I paid. This way, customers were charged only for what they bought. Once the credit card diners got to the front of the line, their transaction was actually faster than that of people who paid with cash. Over the next couple years, this grew exponentially. People loved the freedom to use their credit cards to buy food at McDonald's. It was a novelty. We were really on the cutting edge. Eventually, I was summoned to the Big Mac Conference Room at McDonald's corporate offices.

The Short View

I have always loved McDonald's and have the highest respect for how the company operates. Over the past twelve years, we've sold truckloads of hamburgers and made a lot of money together. However, I had occasional run-ins with the company from time to time over my little innovations.

On this occasion at the Big Mac Conference Room, I was about to make my first presentation to the president of McDonald's USA, Ed Rensi, about our little "McPlastic" idea out in Colorado Springs. Rensi is a McDonald's icon, a powerful leader. and one of Brent Cameron's corporate rivals. During the 1980s, Brent was the president of some McDonald's restaurants where there was explosive and unprecedented growth. Rensi ran the domestic operations, so there was always a little sibling rivalry with those two. Having come into Brent's camp, I inherited a bit of that rivalry, and I was about to get my first taste. I was waiting for him in this big glass conference room with the officers of McDonald's. At the time I didn't know who they were, but I came to find out that these guys were legends. Some of McDonald's greatest minds were sitting in that room, talking hamburger strategy. Listening to their banter was amazing. I sat completely quiet as these brilliant men discussed some of McDonald's biggest strategic issues of the day. It was a powerful experience. Then Rensi entered the room.

All of a sudden it felt like church, everyone sitting in silence while Rensi took his seat at the head of the table. He asked me to start the presentation. I went through how we innovated the process, created cash and grew our credit card sales. At the end, Rensi made a comment about how he could use this machine to block out his wife's spending on her credit card. He could come into my store and run out the limit so she couldn't charge anything more. "Yeah, I guess you could do that," I said, feeling a little puzzled by the response.

Rensi then shouted over the table, "It'll never work, Steve! So take it outta here!"

"Okay, thanks, Ed," I replied, and started to walk out with my big beige credit card box invention under my arm.

Ed walked out of the conference room, put his arm around me and said, "Son, sorry about the way I treated you in there. But, you know, when I get up in the morning and take a crap, it's on the front page of *The Wall Street Journal*." Here, readers, is where I didn't go the extra mile.

"Excuse me," I said, "but I read *The Wall Street Journal* this morning and there was nothing in there about your bowel movements. Okay? And, let me tell you something else. The fifteen minutes before you got in there, those guys were some of the most inspiring people in the world. Then you come and talk like that to me, and none of them open their mouths. So you ought to think about your management style because you're not getting the best mileage out of them. You have a great day, sir." And I left. Remember the rules of instigation? Not perfectly applied, but I was a work in progress.

Despite Rensi's lack of enthusiasm, we kept using our little machine. I signed over both of my credit card patents to McDonald's in March of 1994. By 1997, small-ticket credit sales grew to a billion-dollar industry that included most fast-food restaurants, movie theaters, coffee houses and other traditionally cash-only outlets. It finished at $49 billion in 2005 and continues to grow exponentially. You see, others realized the two barriers to scale here were speed and cost, so lots of people have figured out how to innovate through this method as well. In addition to the industry transformation, this story is also an excellent demonstration of not allowing others to squelch your dream, not to take "no" for an answer. I knew what the customer wanted, and Rensi's opposition to the idea was just an inconvenient obstacle.

Made For You – The Clear View

Now, I've had the privilege of being involved in almost every major innovation at McDonald's in the last 10 years. In the mid-90s, we were in the middle of developing the Made for You operating platform. Before that time, burgers sat pre-made in a warming bin. You'd come in and say, "I want a cheeseburger with no pickles."

Then we'd say, "If God would've wanted you to have a cheeseburger without pickles, he would've made it that way," or "Pull them off yourself."

Not really, but if you're old enough to remember, you know how it was! Made for You was the reinvention of an entire production system, which afforded McDonald's the opportunity to expand its menu and do it in a customized fashion. Now customers could have what they wanted, made the way they wanted. Really an amazing deal.

We had spent six months in the first Made for You store, and we replaced every subsystem in the restaurant. This restaurant had been through a tremendous amount of turmoil and had a lot of turnover. It was breakneck development. On day 11, we ripped out the brains of the restaurant, the point-of-sale system, and on day 12 we opened with a new one. My grills weren't right, the meat wasn't cooking perfectly, so we ordered two new ones. FedEx put those grills, weighing as much as a VW bus, on a plane one day, and we got them the next. We were doing things so quickly! Well, during that time, a McDonald's executive showed up at the restaurant to see how things were going. Of course, I explained to him all the changes we were making. And then I made the mistake of disclosing that there were still some things I wasn't happy with … and I showed him what they were. I pointed underneath the grill, which needed some attention, and said, "You know, the detail to cleanliness isn't what I want it to be." I pointed him to a few other examples. I was letting him know that these things hadn't passed our notice, that we were working on them.

This executive took the liberty of calling the big bosses and telling them that there were "problems" down in my store. In addition, I was about to have a grand opening party that weekend for another store, a brand new Made for You restaurant. Well, McDonald's is diligent about following up with problems, so as soon as that phone call was made I got a parade—and I'm not talking a clown and the Hamburglar. I got a parade of McDonald's people to help me with my "problems." One of the members of this parade was a guy named Don Thompson. Don was being "fast-tracked" for an executive position, but he was a field service manager when I met him. Field service managers are responsible for making sure restaurants adhere to McDonald's standards, and mine was one of his stores.

So Don pulled up in my parking lot and the first words out of his mouth were, "How can I help?" I was in no mood for a parade, so I immediately said, "Oh, that SOB who was here, he called you, huh?" Don calmly said, "Yeah, but let's not focus on that, let's focus on what you need. I'm yours. My staff is yours. Whatever you need to fix this problem, we'll do it." That stopped me cold.

I said, "You know, Don, I really appreciate your willingness to roll up your sleeves and do whatever it takes.

You're doing everything you can to set up an environment where I can be successful." Then I said, "If I need you and all these other people to help me clean a restaurant, then McDonald's has much bigger problems. This new operating system—it will never work."

Don said, "Okay. I suppose you're right. You let me know if you need anything." Then he turned, got into his car and drove back to Denver—the single best thing he could have done for me. Now I don't mean to imply that he wasn't there when I needed him, but at a breakneck time, I needed people to get off my back and give me air cover. And that's exactly what he did. A lesser manager would have come in there with 20 people and taken on the mission to make his mark.

So the restaurant opened. Joe Johnson was the manager. Over the course of a year, that store trained hundreds of staff. It saw nearly 3,000 visitors from 50-odd countries and is one of the key reasons why the Made for You operating system is used today in the US.

And the story behind the story is that Don Thompson, now president of McDonald's USA, had the insight to step back—because he knew the hard work had been done in advance. Don's leadership was visionary because he knew exactly when he needed to get involved and when he didn't, despite being told by a level of management, probably eight or ten players above him, that he needed to unscrew this "problem."

The Long View

Brent Cameron was a smart man who died an untimely death in an avalanche while hiking up one of Colorado's 14,000-foot mountains. It was his dream to climb all 53 "fourteeners," and he died climbing number 39. Before he owned his first restaurant, as president of the international division of McDonald's, Brent was a legend in the company. The international division was the "fair-haired boy" of McDonald's. Brent's game plan all along was to retire in Colorado Springs as a franchisee. But, unlike most franchisees, he didn't want to live in his restaurants shaking hands and fries. He wanted someone to do that for him but realized they would need the incentive of ownership in order to run great restaurants. So, when Brent was the vice president of real estate and legal for McDonald's in the early 1970s, he developed a little loophole that eventually allowed him to give me an equity stake in the restaurants. It wasn't until after he died that McDonald's realized what a problem they had on their hands. I legally owned a share of Brent's stores, but hadn't gone through the traditional franchisee process. Even in death, Brent's vision transcended the party-line mentality.

The year after Brent's death was very difficult for me on many levels. But at the end of it, I was able to buy one store and continue to operate the other stores for Brent's estate. The agreement with McDonald's required the estate to sell the stores to people other than me. So at the end of all of this, I went from managing 11 McDonald's, down to operating just one. Over the next ten years, I acquired 11 more franchises before selling them all in 2006.

Having the Right View

If you're a manager, don't discourage your subordinates. The right view fosters the environment for interactive relationships and innovation. That's the view of visionary leaders like Brent Cameron and Don Thompson. I would also add Mike Roberts, previously the chief operating officer for McDonald's Corporation.

When I worked with a team to develop a new call center to streamline and expedite drive-thru transactions, Mike consistently provided excellent support and direction to the project. He fostered an environment of innovation and excellence and always recognized the accomplishments of others. Mike collaborated better than anyone I ever met and his leadership made the way for the biggest reversal of fortune in McDonald's. He kept me going at McDonald's, and his leadership doubled my net worth, allowing me to pursue *my* vision! McDonald's, like most restaurants, are sold on the basis of cash flow. Mike's leadership grew the cash flow of the system to record levels. And we know a rising tide lifts all the boats!

Innovating the Box

Leveraging innovation as a strategy is easier than it seems. Lots of people confuse innovation with invention. There are very few true inventors out there. Most of us are just building on the ideas of others. Sure, the results of innovation are often a new invention, like the McPlastic machine, but they come from new combinations of existing technology. I didn't invent the software or hardware—I just found someone who could combine those into a new tool. Here's how it's done:

1)   Start with a problem or opportunity.

Take something that frustrates you, your friends, your family, your employees, or anyone, really. Make sure lots of people share your point of view. There are hundreds of innovations that miss this point and therefore never make it into widespread production or use. One example of this principle comes from the *Wallace and Gromit* cartoons. In these little animated movies, the main character is an eccentric British man who creates all sorts of impractical inventions—including a machine that puts your socks on for you and one that lathers and shaves your face. These have no widespread appeal, beyond the character's own eccentric lifestyle. Good innovations start with a common problem that many people share.

2) Look for current approaches to similar problems.

In other words, don't reinvent the wheel if you don't have to. These problems don't have to be in your field: they can come from almost anywhere. Chances are you can find someone who has devised an approach to a similar problem. This will help you to frame your situation while simultaneously exploring practical solutions that might actually help you solve your challenge. When I created the McPlastic machine, I was borrowing technology from full-service restaurants. They already solved part of my problem. I didn't need to create the software that allowed people to authorize their own credit cards: I just needed to see how it could apply to the McDonald's restaurant. Look outside your industry at how other companies are solving similar problems. One of the ways Google keeps its creative employees engaged is to give them one day to themselves to spend time however they wish. They can read a book, go sea kayaking or just sit in the park. The underlying idea is that this time will improve creativity. Maybe you can't give all your people a day each week, but look for the principles in how Google management approached this problem. They took a common issue—the difficulty of inspiring creativity in the office—and married it with a simple solution: giving people time to get inspired in their own ways.

3) Consider "bundling" your solutions.

Like the McPlastic machine, my fast-food call center grew out of another challenge. I had long been concerned about the linear service delivery model in the restaurant business in the mid-1990s. My friend, Tom Ryan, introduced me to the McDiner concept. It was a brilliant idea with great food. I visited the first prototype stores where, instead of waiting in line for their food, people would sit down and order on a little red phone at their tables. (I fell in love with those red plastic phones too!) Their food was prepared to order and delivered straight to their table. I was crazy about the idea—but thought there could be a better implementation. McDiner needed to be integrated with the overall service delivery model. After realizing this, I embarked on a multi-year journey to find a software company to integrate the phone solution with existing drive-thru service. The eventual result was my idea to put the drive-thru order-taker somewhere outside the restaurant—at a call center serving multiple restaurants. It ended up cutting errors and speeding up service. It was simple, but a lot of work.

A little company known as 3Com was inspired by an ambitious airplane inspection employee who used a large electronic clipboard to log reports on plane maintenance and safety. When he used the clipboard, it was massive—the size of a legal notepad. The convergence of this idea with technology that was getting smaller helped create the PDA and a little company called Palm. Now that's innovation.

You can do it, and it's not that hard. In fact, I bet right now you could come up with three innovations by looking at the stuff around you and coming up with ways that it could run better, faster or smarter. Remember, it's what you do with the box you've got! So now, get up off your ... You know the drill-go!

Chapter 4-1/2

There Are No Coincidences

Over these last three chapters, I've illustrated a number of concepts with stories from my past. Other than knowing more about me, you may be thinking, "What does this have to do with being a transformational leader?" I'm so glad you asked. I want to pull all these together into some lessons about practical leadership that will frame the remainder of this book. Those concepts, which are also the titles of the next ten chapters, include:

Vision Attracts Talent

Brent Cameron saw into the future with surprising clarity and accuracy. More importantly, that vision ultimately helped him attract top talent, as it does for all great leaders in their respective fields. Practical leaders envision and cultivate the future they want to live in.

You Must Be Present to Win

Remember my story about fixing the machine in the J&J plant? In order to be a successful leader, you've got to be present when it counts. And, you've got to translate that presence into action. Fixing that machine was a big win for those hard-working J&J plant employees. You can't score those wins if you're not around. You know, that didn't take a tremendous amount of effort on my part—but I was committed to those hard-working factory workers. You've got to be present, ready to work hard and passionately committed.

Collaboration and Teamwork

On Coach Bill Quinn's team, there were no individuals. We all worked together for the good of the whole. As a leader, you need to focus on how to build collaborative team-based strategies to achieve your vision.

Serving Your Guts Out

When my daughter Sara was born, I knew I'd be serving my heart out for this little girl for the rest of my life. I learned that from my dad, Gene, a guy who set aside his own needs to keep our family together. My wife, Brenda, went all the way around the world to adopt two of the children God intended for us. She lives every day as a servant. If you think being successful is about being served by others, you've got the wrong book. You've got to serve...always.

This Is Not a Frat

You know, I thought that by leaving Brown, I'd end up back at the University of Wisconsin—probably in a fraternity house. But once I got to West Point, I realized the Army was not a frat. Guess what? Neither is your business. There's a time and place for fraternity-like camaraderie. But if the upperclassmen at West Point had treated us like frat brothers, I'd have missed a huge character lesson. You've got to like your employees. You just don't want to get drunk and light couches on fire with them.

You Can't Take "No" for an Answer

If I had accepted Rensi's opinion of my McPlastic idea, I might still be scrubbing urinals. Seriously, leaders don't take "no" for an answer. They find a way around it—usually by asking the question, "Why not?"

48

Taking Risks

I wanted to leave J&J to come work for Brent, but it was a huge risk. I took a pay cut, and within weeks I was scrubbing urinals. That risk was the only path to the reward of one day owning 12 McDonald's restaurants. You've got to take risks to be a successful leader.

Ready, Fire, Aim!

I believe in the action-driven life. When I had my outburst with Ed Rensi, I didn't think it through; I just acted on my gut feeling. Over the years, no other behavior has brought me more pain. However, as a leader, you have to focus on an action-driven life. Recall the Action Principle…get up and do something, anything! Error by commission is forgivable; by error by omission is inexcusable. You can never get your wasted time back.

You Can't Put Perfume on a Pig

West Point and the Army changed my life forever. I went in a pig, and came out a man. They don't just dress you up, they break you down and rebuild you in their own image. Friends, being a leader means seeing the world with brutal honesty and knowing what it is going to take to get a job done.

Transformational Leadership

Brent Cameron found a creative, legal and ethical way to circumvent McDonald's rules and make me part-owner in his franchises. That involved creative thinking and long-term vision. Like the Apple ads say: "Think different." It's what leaders do.

You can find great examples of the principles of practical leadership in each of these chapters. They are the ingredients that have made up my life to this point. What about you—are you ready to jump into the kitchen of life? The next ten chapters will give you ingredients to mix, layer, toss or add at just the right time to create a unique vision for your future. You might have to get your hands dirty: All good cooks do.

Chapter 5

Vision Attracts Talent

A leader is one who knows the way,
goes the way, and shows the way.

John Maxwell

On my second birthday, April 20, 1961, President John F. Kennedy sent a memo to his vice president, Lyndon Johnson, posing one very important question: Is there a milestone in space exploration where the United States could beat the Soviet Union?

Just days before this memo, the Soviet cosmonaut Yuri Gagarin had become the first man in space. America was falling behind the Soviet Union in every major space accomplishment. Furthermore, Kennedy was humiliated by the recent failure of the Bay of Pigs invasion of Cuba. Faced with a series of upstart communist revolutions throughout Southeast Asia, failure to contain communism in our own hemisphere and losing the space race, Kennedy believed he needed to do something dramatic, and he needed to do it soon.

Out of this investigation, the Kennedy administration decided that a manned mission to the moon was a battle the US could win. One month later, Kennedy addressed a joint session of Congress to declare, "I believe that this nation should commit itself to achieving the goal, before this decade is out,

51

of landing a man on the moon and returning him safely to the Earth."[6]Congress agreed and passed the resolution authorizing funding for this ambitious space program, costing more than $9 billion in 1960s dollars.

Critics attacked the program immediately. They claimed it was too vast, too expensive and too great a drain on our scientific resources. They were right, but they didn't catch the greater point: The only way to beat the Soviets was to marshal every ounce of our resources and apply them toward a singular, massive scientific and technological achievement. We needed a catapult to launch us ahead of the Soviets and establish the United States as the leader in space exploration. Guiding this program was Kennedy's vision of Americans walking around on the moon. I wonder if he dreamed about them driving their moon buggies, teeing off from the American flag and hitting golf balls into the infinite darkness of space. The vision had pragmatic political roots, but I know Kennedy could see it in his mind's eye. Fortunately, most of America could as well, and you know how the story ends, with the Apollo mission.

Your Own Personal Apollo

Do you have an Apollo program in your life? What can you picture yourself doing or becoming? I didn't have a clear vision for my life until I met Brent Cameron. Sometimes you need someone in your life who helps you crystallize your vision. Kennedy had Johnson, NASA staff and a team of advisors behind him. In this chapter, I'm going to help you understand and apply some key concepts about vision to your everyday life:

1) Vision describes your preferred future.
2) Vision motivates your behavior.
3) Vision thrives on community.
4) Vision attracts talent.

This is very similar to the process we described in Chapter 1 about defining and refining your dream. But there's a big component of this chapter that focuses on how to use vision as a magnet to attract talent. First, another warning:

DON'T CONFUSE THE TOOLS YOU NEED WITH YOUR END RESULT.

Sometimes people become so enamored with the process, they forget the destination altogether. This can lead to "hammer vision."

Hammer Vision: Losing the Big-Picture Focus

Think with me for a minute. If your vision is to build an entire house, would you spend all your resources on your hammer? Of course not. The hammer is one tool that helps the vision—but it is not the house. The same is true of money, power, and influence. Many people mistake these for ends in themselves. Like the hammer, these are tools to achieve a vision.

Pursuing Self-Interest: Bank on Your Preferred Future

When Kennedy attempted a large-scale space exploration project to beat the Soviets, he knew this was in the country's and his own best interest. He committed a lot— money, political capital, manpower, and time—to his grand pursuit. Here's the bottom line: **We commit our resources to things that are important to us.** Some of the smartest economists in the universe believe that all of human behavior is tied to the pursuit of self- interest.

I believe in the old saying, made famous recently by author Stephen Covey in *The 7 Habits of Highly Effective People*, "Begin with the end in mind."

That's all vision is, really. It's your definition of a preferred future—for yourself, your company, your family. We all have a concept of what our preferred future looks like, even if we're not aware of it. Let me use my kids as an example: My vision for them is pretty concrete. It includes their getting good grades in school, finishing college, getting a good job, and starting a family. When I communicate those expectations to my children, they also begin to also see a vision for their lives. Over the years, I've seen them fill in the blanks of that vision with report cards, college acceptance letters, resumes, offer letters, and so on. All of these are reminders of how the vision is coming together.

Let me give you another example of what a preferred future looks like. When I was at West Point, my vision was to become an upperclassman and graduate. The upperclassmen were actual representations of that vision. I could look at their faces and say, "That will be me in three years."

When you have this vision, you know what you want to accomplish. But more importantly, you know what you are *not* going to accomplish. If your vision is to become CEO of your company, then you probably shouldn't quit your job. With the end in mind, your can order your behavior. Think of it as a fixed point in the future that is pulling you closer and closer with each passing day. And passionate leaders, real visionaries, are like magnetic forces that draw you in—other people can't help but catch their vision and want to be a part of it. Did you get that? Your job is to motivate people to adopt your vision of the future as their own act of self-interest.

You've heard it said that people are motivated by money and power, but I'm telling you that people are motivated by ownership in a compelling vision to make a difference. This isn't just Pollyanna talk. In fact, I believe Bill Gates is the richest man in the world because he understands the power of vision to attract talent and motivate performance. Gates used his vision to create a world where the global economy is dependent on Microsoft's software.

Leader's Exercise

Take a few minutes and write down your preferred future. Using the information we have about your dream from Chapter 1, we're now going to make it concrete. Imagine it's twenty years from today: What does your future look like? Your family, job, leisure time—the works. If you know you'll be retired in twenty years, then write an article about what you've accomplished. Perhaps you think you'll be dead in twenty years, so write your own eulogy and obituary. Maybe this statement is only one sentence: "Put a man on the moon by the end of the 1960s," or "Every computer in the world will run on Windows software." Write a novel if that is what it takes. Do it in your own way! Remember, there are lots of paths to take you to your dream.

Bill Gates: Vision Personified

Typing the words "Bill Gates" into Google gets you about 44 million hits. By comparison, "Jesus Christ" brings up about 59 million, "Abraham Lincoln" 14 million, and "Brett Favre" just 1.8 million. "Steve Bigari" gets 10,600.[8] The richest man in the world gets a lot of press. Everyone wants to know how Bill Gates built his software empire and what he's going to do next. For all his money, Gates is a guy who loves computers and has an enormous vision for how they can change human behavior. The money Gates has made is just a byproduct of the vision.

Gates' vision was a little nuts. It all started with a couple of geeks in a garage back in the 1970s. Describing the early days of Microsoft, Gates said, "We didn't even obey a 24-hour clock. We'd come in and program for a couple of days straight. We'd—you know, four or five of us—when it was time to eat we'd all get in our cars, kind of race over to the restaurant and sit and talk about what we were doing, sometimes I'd get excited talking about things, I'd forget to eat, but then you know, we'd just go back and program some more. It was us and our friends—those were fun days."[9] Real vision changes behavior. It's a lot like love. Time becomes irrelevant, eating takes a back seat, and we are infused with an almost superhuman drive. I love that first line, "We didn't even obey a 24-hour clock...." Doesn't that say so much?

As Americans, we're slaves to the clock. Right now, there are no fewer than three different clocks within my line of sight. They stand watch over us, telling us when it's appropriate to work, eat, sleep, and play. Truthfully, time is our most precious commodity. An ancient Chinese proverb says, "An inch of time is worth an inch of gold, but an inch of gold cannot buy an inch of time." When our time is lost, we can't buy it back with all the money in Bill Gates' investment account. But when a vision captures our hearts, it is more compelling than time itself. Gates also talks about being excited with friends. He didn't do it alone. His high school buddy, Paul Allen, was there with him, along with a couple of other guys who really bought into the vision that what they were doing could make a difference.

One of the other things we are taught as we are growing up is that Americans are rugged individualists. It's woven into our cultural identity, and the fabric of the American dream itself. People don't think of Microsoft without envisioning Bill Gates. Think of other companies you know and I bet you'll find there is a prominent name or face that pops into your mind. Even if you don't know that person's name, you can probably figure out what the vision is that drives him or her. It's just the way we're wired. But Gates didn't build Microsoft by himself; he had a team—we might call them nerds—staying up all night to write software code. Today, we call them the world's richest men. Buying into a vision is fun because it's community oriented.

BIGG IDEA: VISION ATTRACTS TALENT.

Vision Attracts Talent

Talent, by the way, is an extremely rare commodity these days. I can teach you how to make burgers, but I can't teach you talent. As I explained earlier, great vision transfers the passion of your heart into the hearts of others. I think Gates and Microsoft were masterful at this. At some level, Gates wanted all Microsoft employees to feel the rush of staying up all night, forgetting to eat, and watching action movies with friends when they needed a break from programming. Now that Microsoft is all grown up, it has more sophisticated problems with its 60,000-plus employees.[10]

Back in December 2005, Microsoft went mining for new talent in India. Knowing that it was competing against other world-class companies for the same Indian programmers, Microsoft innovated an idea called "Code4Bill." Essentially, Microsoft enticed Indian programmers to apply to the company by inviting them to enter a programming contest in which the top prize was a job with Bill Gates' personal software development team. Think of it as "The Apprentice" for geeks. But I never heard the Donald ask a question like:

An array contains 9 occurrences of 0s, 8 occurrences of 1s and 7 occurrences of 2s in any order. The array is to be sorted using only swap operations. What is the minimum number of swaps needed in the worst case to sort the array?

I love this idea because it inspires these Indian programmers to dream about working alongside Bill Gates. It's gimmicky and fun, but it really hits on a core principle. Microsoft knows that its competitive advantage lies in the vision of Bill Gates. Microsoft is counting on the fact that others want to get as close as possible to that vision. So they innovated that fact into a contest to inspire thousands, maybe millions, of people to want to work for Microsoft.

You'd think that with all of Microsoft's dominance, Gates would be ready for a break. He recently stepped out of day-to-day operations at Microsoft, but the vision persists. Just a few years ago, Gates said, "We haven't even come close to fulfilling the basic dream of the personal computer." I bet Gates sees computers used in new, creative and different ways around the world. I know he sees a brighter future for the two billion of our global neighbors who live in poverty. He's pursuing his next dream, and I applaud him in his desire to do for social issues, like poverty, what he did for personal computing.

When Visions Fail

This book is about practical leadership, but there is a big part of vision that is a little impractical. Men on the moon? Total dominance of the personal computing market? These things can sound a little crazy depending on the context. And my advice to you is to always set your vision within the bounds of your current context and circumstances. For example, let's say my vision was to play for the Green Bay Packers. It causes me pain to admit that's—probably—never going to happen. The context is all wrong. In reality, I no longer possess the physical characteristics necessary to play professional football. That vision is out. Think big, but consider your vision in the realm of possibility.

Practical Ideas for Practical Leaders

Just two things you need to remember here: Refine and communicate.

1)   Refine the vision.

Make your vision clear and concise by developing three different versions. First, articulate it in one complete sentence. Make it as simple to understand as possible. This is the snappy answer you'll give when someone says, "So what do you do?" "I help working families attain the highest levels of prosperity possible," is my reply. You also need the "elevator" version. Unless you're in a New York skyscraper, the average time spent in an elevator is under a minute. You need a version that can easily be related in an elevator or another very short period of time. Finally, you need a three-minute version—something appropriate for a TV interview. Louis Pasteur said, "Chance favors the prepared mind."[11] Having three versions of your vision helps you deal with a variety of situations and circumstances.

2) Communicate the vision.

The reason you spend so much time refining your vision is so you can share it with others. You can't attract talent if you aren't able to clearly communicate your vision. In fact, you want to relentlessly share it with anyone willing to listen to you. This increases your chances of getting heard by someone who can make a difference. Share your vision with confidence and passion.

I conceived the off-site call center as part of my vision for a "parallel service delivery model," or taking food orders from any point inside or outside the restaurant. But I ran into one critical problem. I was unable to find a software company that could sequence cars in the drive-thru lane using digital pictures. This was a key piece of my vision—and I made sure everyone knew it. So I had hundreds of people contacting me about this or that software company. After dozens of meetings that ended in failure, I came up with a rule that I would look only at companies that had three or more references. This led me to a Boston-based company called Exit 41 and a man named Craig Tengler. I met Craig in Denver and asked him the $1 million question: "Can your software sequence cars in the drive-thru using digital photos?"

Without blinking, Craig said, "Yeah, we actually put it in our last software release but no one wanted it, so we pulled it for the most recent one. Why?"

I told him, "I'll ask the questions," and this was the beginning of a lifelong friendship.

Exit 41 helped me achieve the call center vision. Unfortunately I had to kiss a lot of frogs before finding the prince, but that's okay. If you're not willing to kiss those frogs, you really have no passion. During those years, I talked to anyone who could possibly have helped me. And I didn't expect them to see my whole vision. They just had to get the part about sequencing cars using digital photos.

You'll rarely find a silver-bullet approach to your vision; achieving it means cobbling it together piece by piece. When I talked about a parallel service delivery model, people thought I was really crazy—probably the way that people thought about Bill Gates in the early years.

The Power of Vision

Vision motivates human behavior in powerful ways. Bill Gates is an excellent model for what we are talking about. But maybe you don't believe you have a vision as big or compelling as his. Truth is, not many do. And that's fine—you need *your* vision. I met Steve Case on my last Ashoka interview. Ashoka (www. ashoka.org) is a world-changing group of social entrepreneurs founded by Bill Drayton, one of the greatest visionary leaders of our time. Steve Case departed AOL on his own quest to transform health care. I know it's the stickiest wicket of our time, but don't underestimate him! Steve said, *"You're not as talented as they think you are when you're on top, nor as bad as they think when you fail."*

Gates claims he still knows the original programming code for his first PC by heart.[12] I bet you've got something knocking around in your head right now. I can't tell you what it is. Maybe it's a vision for being a better boss, learning how to become a better parent, or doubling your productivity. What quickens your heart? When you embrace that, you're going to start behaving and acting differently. I promise, if you define that vision and keep making it clearer and clearer, your vision will attract the talent you need to see it accomplished.

61

Chapter 6

~~~~~~~

You Must Be Present to Win

You're never guaranteed about next year. People ask
what you think of next season;
you have to seize the opportunities
when they're in front of you.

Brett Favre

I was born in the mining town of Iron River in the Upper Peninsula of Michigan. When the iron business finally dried up, most of the town's industry and economy died. My dad, Gene, decided that it was time for our family to seek better opportunities, so he packed us up, moved our family to Milwaukee and took a job as a salesman. There's very little to do in Michigan's Upper Peninsula except throw snowballs at one another, so you get very close to football, especially the Green Bay Packers. When I was a young boy, I watched the legends play. I saw the Packers win the first two Super Bowls. My childhood heroes were guys like Vince Lombardi, Bart Starr and Ray Nitschke. These giants of the game inspired me. What I didn't realize at the time was that I was living with the greatest hero in my life, my dad.

My dad was working a sales job for Gimbel's department store in Milwaukee, and he would put in tons of overtime and extra hours just to win the sales contests. The prize was tickets to go see the Packers play a game down at Milwaukee County Stadium. We could never even imagine getting tickets for Lambeau Field. In fact, I was an adult before I was able to afford the tickets to watch a game on the Packers' home field. Ironically, my dad was a Detroit Lions fan. He hated the Packers! But he knew how much my brothers and I loved the games, so he did whatever it took to get us there. He had to work a lot. When he wasn't at work, he was with us. He started going to my football games when I played for the General Lumber Saints when I was six years old. I can't remember a game he didn't attend.

It took a tremendous amount of courage for us to leave Iron River and move to Milwaukee. Before moving, my dad was the manager of a hardware store that was slowly declining as the mines started closing. Making matters worse, my mother worked as a nurse and severely injured her back on the job. In fact, after the injury she never was able to return to work. She never truly recovered. It's one reason why today I'm such a stickler on worker's compensation issues. I once told a kid that even if he was on a respirator, I'd put him to work.

The doctors who treated my mom took her life 28 years before it ended. Through their advice, she ended up addicted to prescription drugs and never found her way back to any type of productive work. It was a horrible three decades for her and our family, and it put an enormous financial and emotional strain on all of us. But through this experience, my dad stuck with us. He stayed with my mom. He was our rock. Because of my dad, I was able to overcome my anger and frustration with her. Because of him, I could sit at her bedside during the final moments of her life and truly reconnect with her—an amazing gift.

No, packing us up for Milwaukee wasn't easy. My extended family lived in the Upper Peninsula, and it was rare for people to move away with spouse and kids to take a better-paying job. But my dad knew that's what needed to be done, and he never looked back. As a kid, I never knew the extent of his sacrifice for us. You hear stories about men who leave their families when they hit troubled times. But that's not part of who he is. Better than anyone I know, my dad—Gene Bigari—knew that you must be present to win.

I can't think about my dad or my younger days without thinking of football. It was a big part of our life. Like many Wisconsin boys, I dreamed that someday I'd become a Green Bay Packer. Today, I still dream about what that would have been like. I still "suit up" in green and yellow from time to time when I watch a game. In my forty-year journey with football, I've seen some tremendous ups and downs. But the main character of one of the greatest chapters of the Green Bay Packer legacy is a guy who replicates my dad's qualities on the field, and that's quarterback Brett Favre. At the close of the 2006 season, here were some of Favre's career stats and records take from www. packers.com:

- Second in career passing yards (57,500)
- Second in career passing attempts (8,223)
- First in career pass completions (5,021)
- Second in career touchdown passes (414)
- Tied for second in career wins as a starting quarterback (147)
- Third in consecutive games started (237)

If Farve continues to stay healthy, he will almost certainly move into the number one position for many of those records, and pass Dan Marino as one of the most prolific quarterbacks NFL history. But, in addition to all these fantastic accomplishments, he may also break the all-time interception record pretty soon.

That's because he never quits! What I admire most about Favre is that he's a blue-collar, lunch-pail kind of guy. He comes to work every day to get the snot knocked out of him, just so he can be present in the last two minutes of the game. He spends 58 minutes getting his teeth rattled around his helmet so he can be there to win the game when everything is on the line. That, to me, is a fun guy to watch because it's not about the money, the fame or the records—it's just about playing the game. At no time was that more evident than on December 22, 2003.

The day before, Favre's father, Irvin Favre, had died of a massive heart attack, and Brett was preparing for a Monday Night Football match-up between the Packers and the Oakland Raiders. No one expected Favre to play, assuming he'd return to Kiln, Mississippi, to be with his family during this time of grief. So when the team announced that Favre would start the game, many criticized that decision. When the Packers took the field that night, Favre was a man possessed. By the end of the game, Favre had thrown for 399 yards and four touchdowns in the 41-7 rout of the Raiders. Overcome with tears and emotion, Favre said after the game: "I knew that my dad would have wanted me to play. I love him so much, and I love this game. It's meant a great deal to me, to my dad, to my family, and I didn't expect this kind of performance. But I know he was watching tonight."[13]

Throughout his career, Favre has been the consummate field general, leading the Packers to many fourth-quarter wins and snatching victory from his opponents at the last minute—even the last seconds. But what amazes me most about the night Favre delivered the performance that became a fitting eulogy for his father is that he couldn't have done it alone. Yes, he showed up for the game, reliable Brett suiting up in the midst of tragedy, but it took Favre's inspired teammates to make the rest happen that Monday night in Oakland. As you watch the highlights, you can't help but notice that the players caught everything he threw. They elevated their game to meet Brett's leadership. This is the hallmark of leadership and teamwork—and those moments happened because Favre chose to show up.

This story illustrates the similarities between Brett Favre on the field and Gene Bigari, my dad, in my life. My dad has always "shown up" for me. For my dad's 75th birthday, I might just take him to a Packers game to celebrate. It's not *his* team, but I think he'd come. And in spite of the fact that he's never gotten over the Lions, my dad is still my hero.

Being Present to Win

This is probably one of the simplest ideas in this entire book to implement right now. Even quirky filmmaker Woody Allen gets this idea. "Eighty percent of success is showing up," Allen says.[14] Actually, I'd go even further to say that sometimes, 100 percent of success is just showing up. There's something about this idea that many people still don't understand. You can't do it by remote control. "Calling it in" is not good enough. Unfortunately, lots of people think that it is. We "outsource" the raising of our kids to daycare centers, sports coaches and teachers. Business leaders flee the office rather than spend time connecting and relating with their employees. Technology further separates us. We write e-mails instead of making phone calls. Conference calls and videoconferencing replace face-to-face contact. How many times have you seen a conference speaker with an asterisk beside his name that says "invited?" I see it all the time, and I really wonder if it's a valuable technique. Inviting the headline speaker isn't success...getting him to show up is! None of these things is bad; they just make it more challenging to "be present" in the lives of other people.

There's an old concept known as "management by walking around" (MBWA). Back in the 1930s, Dave Packard and Bill Hewlett went on a camping trip in Colorado that became the basis of their long-term friendship and business partnership. They started the company that became Hewlett Packard (HP) in a garage in Palo Alto, California.[15]Their first products were instruments designed to test sound equipment, and Walt Disney was one of their first customers. As the company grew throughout the 1940s and 1950s, David Packard created MBWA. Packard said, "I learned that quality requires minute attention to every detail, that everyone in an organization wants to do a good job, that written instructions are seldom adequate, and that personal involvement needs to be frequent, friendly, unfocused and unscheduled—but far from pointless. And since its principal aim is to seek out people's thoughts and opinions, it requires good listening." At the same time, HP established an "open-door policy" throughout the company. The founders instilled the expectation that managers would be available, open and receptive to inquiries from their subordinates. Taken together, MBWA and the open-door policy helped establish a strong mutual trust and understanding throughout HP's workforce.

This seems downright old-fashioned in the age of the Internet. What can walking around do that e-mail can't? Packard understood that by walking around, you could actually be present in the lives of your coworkers. Part of the corporate legend is that all engineers and designers were supposed to have their projects out and ready for comment by anyone else in the company. Through this planned spontaneity, many of HP's greatest innovations were born. But MBWA requires people to actually *be present*! You cannot send an e-mail, fax, instant message, or text message—you have to be there to ask and answer questions, provide insight and remove barriers for others. Technology is a great tool, but a horrible management and leadership strategy. There is no such thing as "management by e-mail." E-mail should be used only to convey facts, arrange meetings and save time. Never try to have a conversation by e-mail. Instead, get away from your computer screen. Remember, the view from behind your desk is very incomplete and will keep you from seeing the big picture. To get it, you've got to go out and find it. This requires—say it with me—"being present."

Many of the people who work with me have the misconception that being present to win requires them to sacrifice their personal and family time. Work and family are not mutually exclusive, and both of them require your presence. I didn't get it when Sara, my oldest daughter, was growing up. I was entirely too focused on work. But as I've gotten older, I've come to realize that you can do both. You don't always have to work a 70-hour week. When you do, it gets to be a habit. Like any bad habit, it's hard to kick. When I put in long hours now, I'm really missing my wife, Brenda, and the kids. Work never becomes a replacement for my family life. It's a shame we've set up work and family as mortal enemies when all you really need to do to balance the two is develop good discernment. You've got to know when your presence is absolutely necessary and when it is not.

One way to do this is to look at the consequences of your decision over short, medium, and long-term timeframes. Can you believe that I am going to steal an idea from *O The Oprah Magazine*? In an article featured in *O*, Suzy Welch talks about making decisions, great and small, using the 10-10-10 method. I think it's a pretty good system. When you need to make a decision about something in your life, ask yourself: What will the consequences be in 10 minutes, 10 months, and 10 years?

It's another way to look at the urgent versus the important. The great thing about this tool is that it's easy to remember and allows you to quickly evaluate consequences over a broad spectrum of time. Once you've evaluated the impact, you can make a much better decision—and better explain that decision to others.[16]

By going through this process, you won't stay a minute longer than you need to in order to get the job done. You'll be far more focused at work when you're at work, and at home when you're at home. This will also improve the quality of the time you spend at both places. Showing up is important, but showing up at the right time, for the right amount of time, is really what you are after.

But showing up isn't the end of the story. There's an interesting phenomenon in American work life called presenteeism. The term applies to employees showing up sick, injured, or in some other way not prepared to work or those who put in excessive hours at work, but who aren't really working—like the employee who wants to give his boss the impression of working hard, but he's actually playing Spider Solitaire on his computer. He's present, but not all there. This can happen anywhere, but it's highly documented in the workplace. Presenteeism costs American companies billions of dollars each year. Think of how presenteeism could be fixed in a company with MBWA, open-door policies, and employees independently making decisions using a tool like 10-10-10. I'd like to believe it would go away completely. The moral here is to make sure that your time spent on the job, any job, is truly quality time. I believe the only way you can discern that is through some decision-making grid like 10-10-10.

BIGG IDEA: YOU MUST BE
PRESENT TO WIN!

Being There To Win

Today, it's common to wear many hats, at our jobs and in our private lives, and it can be overwhelming. We can all be present to win, no matter how many priorities we are juggling. Here are a few guidelines:

1) Get gut-level honest with yourself.

Is there an important area of your life that needs more attention and presence from you? Does it need more quality time, quantity time or both? For those of us with healthy doses of ego, we can't think of a situation that our presence would not improve. There are others who believe they never add anything by their presence. Both share the same root problem—too much thinking about yourself! Get over yourself. Take an honest look at the situation ahead of you and decide if your presence is critical, helpful, unhelpful or detrimental. Show up only for things that fall into the "critical" and "helpful" categories. If you can't decide, ask your coworkers and friends what they think. You'll get some honest feedback about your abilities and contribution.

2) Work isn't everything.

Lots of men and women are driven by their career accomplishments. I already told you that I made this mistake early in my career when Sara was growing up. You have to remember that work is just one part of your life. I believe that most people should love their work, but love their families, hobbies, friendships and personal lives a whole lot more. When you find yourself wanting to stay at work to avoid those other

71

areas of your life, something is wrong. Go see a counselor now! You can be present at work, and still want to be somewhere else. Look no further than Brett Favre for proof of that. He showed up to win on December 22, 2003, but I bet you anything that where he really wanted to be was in Kiln, Mississippi, with his family. You should feel the same way.

3) Consider quality vs. quantity.

Avoid the trap of presenteeism—showing up for showing up's sake. You must be present at the right time where you can apply the greatest amount of leverage to a given situation. There are lots of stay-at-home parents who don't spend much quality time with their kids. That's presenteeism of another kind. When Sara and Cali were growing up, I used to talk on my cell phone a lot. I'd always take a call in the evening or while driving them to school. In my mind, I was at home with the kids doing my fatherly duties. But one day Sara told me, "Dad, you're never really around for us." I pulled the car over because I was so shocked. "What do you mean?" I asked her, and I immediately started chronicling all the time we had spent together. How I always went out of my way to race home to be with them. "Yeah, Dad," said Cali, "but you're not *really* with us. You're always on the phone." I realized I was neither really present nor winning. I had kept score in my family by counting minutes and hours instead of experiences and memories.

In all of this, you've got to remember that when you're present, unexpected things happen that will turn into big wins for you. It's the vacation from hell, when the car breaks down on a moonless night and you have to walk five miles to the nearest exit, that becomes a funny part of your family legacy. It's the football game where you spill hot chocolate on the guy next to you because your hand is frozen to the cup, and he becomes a lifelong friend. It's the visit from your family during the dinner rush at McDonald's that leads to an innovation like McPlastic. It's the fourth-quarter drive that makes all the difference for the game. These things happen all the time and are usually centered on a crisis or a problem. These are the things that make life worth living, but you'll never get to experience them if you're not present.

Strategies to Win

Employing this strategy requires self-knowledge, discipline and setting boundaries. These exercises will help you figure it out:

1) Write a list of every role you play at this point in your life, and rank those roles in order of importance. For the sake of the exercise, if you have a title or label for the role you play (e.g. daddy, boss, member), write it down.

2) Write down how much time you devote to each one. You can write this as a percentage of your available time or in the number of hours you spend in a week, whatever makes the most sense to you.

3) Determine if you are spending too much, not enough, or just the right amount of time on each area. Divide your assessment into quantity and quality time.

4) Look for mismatches between quantity and quality time and make adjustments accordingly.

5) Write up your new list of priorities with target goals for how much time each one needs from you.

6) Come up with some boundaries and rules. For example, in my house, I don't return phone calls or e-mails until the kids are in bed. Every once in a while I will sneak off to respond to an urgent e-mail, but each time I catch myself I become a little better, which leads to the last point...

7) Establish a system of accountability with those who have permission to tell you when you've strayed out of bounds.

Everyone who knows me knows my boundaries. I had an employee leave her keys in my car when we went to a meeting. When she called to tell me about it, she said, "Steve, I'm so sorry to bother you on your cell phone when you're with your family!" She knew I was with my son and about to eat dinner. When I offered to drive the keys down to her, she said, "No, I don't want to take away from your family time. I'll come and get them." Knowing my boundaries helped her solve this problem for herself, and it allowed me to keep my commitment to quality time with my family.

If you have trouble determining how much time you should spend on an activity, use the 10-10-10 decision-making guideline to evaluate the quality of the time you spend.

Chapter 7

Collaboration and Teamwork

*Teamwork is the ability to work together toward a
common vision, the ability to direct individual accomplishments
toward organizational objectives. It is the fuel that allows
common people to attain uncommon results.*

Andrew Carnegie

The Emergency Room of Life

There are 39 million Americans classified as "working poor."[17] You've probably heard that phrase, "working poor." I happen to hate it. Poor is a mentality—not an economic condition. The people we quickly classify as the "working poor" are really *hard-working Americans just like you and me.* They have dreams and passions, and for whatever reasons, the only jobs available to them are entry-level positions, such as those in the fast-food industry. When you think of these great people, I want you to begin seeing them as individuals and families—hard-working men and women who want to make a difference in their lives. There is no such thing as "working poor," because people with the guts to get up every morning and work to provide food, clothing and shelter for their families are anything but poor. No—they are some of the most inspiring people I have ever met. Through them, I have learned a lot about collaboration and teamwork.

It is no secret that fast-food restaurants rely on workers who can quickly learn a simple model of food "production." Because of the relatively low cost of labor, most fast food restaurants have high turnover, 200 to 400 percent per year.[18]Building a good team is hard work; these dynamics make it nearly impossible. It's not uncommon for people to start work and then quit after seeing the size of their first paycheck. "I can get more money on welfare," is what many of them tell us. That kind of turnover was unacceptable to me, so I started looking for the roots of this problem. What I found is no surprise. Those 39 million Americans need the same things we all do: healthcare, transportation, financial planning, housing, computer skills, loans, education and opportunities for advancement. The difference is that our economy doesn't reward a person for having a low-skill job, bad credit and no education. The result is a system that spits out lots of people pursuing the American dream in a game that's rigged against them. Realizing that these motivations are common to all of us, I set out to find a way that I, as a fast-food franchisee, could do my part to help my employees have a better quality of life.

I did a couple of studies when I started America's Family. I considered raising prices to provide what my employees needed, but I would have had to raise prices 400 percent—and I would have lost all my customers. Or I could have given up everything I made, but then my staff would get less than a 50 cent raise. Really—I took every dime I was making and said, "What if I do this work for free?" In reality, who would take millions of dollars worth of risk and work 70-hour weeks for free? Neither idea was practical or fun! I had the inspiration. I only required the instigation and innovation. I had a heart for these folks but no way to solve the problem myself. I knew I needed help from the entire community. From this inspiration American's Family was born (www.amfol.com).

The problem I just described is complex and multifaceted and it is further complicated because the children in these families are trapped in generational poverty. Consider this example: You're a single mom and just one paycheck away from total disaster. You work two jobs. You rent an apartment in a poor neighborhood. You have no car, and the only place you can shop for groceries is 7-Eleven—which costs you twice as much as shopping in Wal-Mart. You have a high school diploma, and the only job you can get is in a low-skill service industry. When your children get sick, you've got no choice but to miss work. You have no bank account, so when you need cash you borrow from a payday lender at over 500 percent interest. After missing work a few times because of "emergency room of life" issues, your employer fires you. So you have to go out and find another low-wage, entry-level job that puts you one paycheck away from this whole scenario. But, you're a boot-strapper, so you go out and make it work. How do you get out of this trap?

I believe this problem can only be resolved through education and relationships. In order to get them, a number of things have to come together. The folks who are "working poor" find themselves that way because they do not have the right education or the right relationships—and don't have the resources to get them either. So, they need to get help from the community, especially from their employers. Most folks see the problem as being one of resources. But typically, that's not the problem.

For instance, in the area of health care, there's no reason on God's earth why any child in America lacks adequate health care coverage. There are literally millions of dollars—real money that exists today—that remain unspent on child health care because the children who need care cannot be found. It's not a resource problem; it's an issue of distribution. What I'm telling you is that there is a fundamental disconnect between the people who need services and those who are able to provide them for low or no cost to the families. To fix this, you need all three sectors—government, business and nonprofit—working together on this issue.

Fundamentally, the problem goes back to the failure of the "Great Society" programs of the 1960s. At that time, the government told us they would take care of the less fortunate in our society. And many churches and businesses said, "Thank God! Somebody else is going to take care of them." The fact is that the problem is so huge, the government alone could never provide all the resources for every impoverished American family. Instead, you need to leverage the power of collaboration and teamwork between the government, private and nonprofit sectors in a new strategy where each party is independently pursuing its vested self-interest. Through this model, we can reach many more families who need help without placing an undue burden on any one area of our economy. It sounds simple because it is.

My first attempt at achieving this level of collaboration was called the "We Care Fair." I invited banks, hospitals, nonprofit organizations, and government service providers to host tables and enroll my employees in their free programs. You see, financial institutions have an interest or requirement to serve people of modest means. States like Colorado have free immunization and healthcare programs for children and poor families. Communities have hundreds of nonprofits that provide vital social services *for free*, but many of them are underutilized.

Why? Information. Many people simply do not know what benefits exist and how to properly access them. The "We Care Fair" brought together all of these service providers in one place. We had no idea what we were getting into.

We packed my parking lot with booths from providers all over the state. Government officials from Denver came down on a Sunday afternoon to enroll kids in the health care program. Loan officers from the local credit union were there. My employees came—and they brought their neighbors, friends, family members and a whole bunch of other people, too.

Not long after this fair, I got a call from Ken Barun, then-CEO of Ronald McDonald House Charities. Joan Kroc—philanthropist and wife of Ray Kroc, McDonald's first franchisee and later Chair of McDonald's Corporation—had just donated $100 million to the Ronald McDonald House Charities, and I was invited to help them figure out how to spend the grant. I said, "Send it to me, and I can spend it over the weekend." That should show you how foolish I am, because it takes a lot more work to give away $100 million than it does to make $100 million. Don't believe me? The world's second-richest guy, Warren Buffett, had to give his fortune to the richest guy in the world, Bill Gates, to figure out how to give it away! Over the next 18 months, I was able to work closely with a team that included McDonald's board member Don Lubin and Ronald McDonald House founder Dr. Audrey Evans in figuring out what to do with these funds. This process culminated with a major presentation in Chicago, where we invited some of the nation's largest charities and foundations to come and give us their pitch on how to spend the grant. What I realized at this event was that even with this $100 million grant, the problem wasn't just money—it was distribution. Most of these places already had the solution figured out, but didn't have the right channels for getting the resources where they needed to go. That's when I began to see the "disconnect" between service provision and service delivery. A better fusion was needed, so we decided to start America's Family as a resource center for low-income families to connect with the free services already available to them.

America's Family works directly with employers and community leaders to help hard-working but impoverished people gain financial skills, access to loans, quality medical coverage and other vital resources. The idea is to help them change their lives by rewarding their hard work and self-sufficiency in ways that help them become better workers, more disciplined consumers and givers rather than takers in their communities. Cooperating employers recruit workers who utilize payroll deductions and develop financial planning skills so they can accumulate the money they need to invest in their own futures. The key to success is our collaborative community partnerships among nonprofits, public agencies and private businesses. Millions of Americans who work at entry-level jobs in the service industries are one paycheck, one medical emergency, or one busted radiator away from financial collapse. Through the wise application of social entrepreneurship, we can help these workers have their first taste of financial security, which is good for employers, too.

Michelle, one of the best employees I've ever had, exemplifies the type of teamwork and collaboration that America's Family creates. Seven years ago, she joined the team as a crew person in one of my McDonald's stores. Her last position before leaving the company was at the desk right outside my office as one of our call center managers. In that role, she operated one of the most sophisticated restaurant software applications in the world. When we created the call center—which is capable of remotely processing fast-food, drive-thru window orders for any restaurant in the world—she was there helping me iron out all the details. She worked day and night alongside my staff and me to make sure we had the most technologically advanced, customer-oriented call center on the planet. She was essential in the innovation of this call center, one that eventually was profiled by *New York Times* reporter Thomas Friedman in *The World is Flat*, a book about the global economy.[19]

Michelle was an invaluable part of my team, and I was excited to show her off when our call center was visited by 30 executives from McDonald's. Reggie Webb orchestrated this visit. He is an operator from Los Angeles and is the best instigator I have ever met. I call him the Martin Luther King, Jr. of McDonald's! These visitors were people from the top leadership of McDonald's, and it was a big deal for us to host them. When they came into the call center, I asked Michelle to give them the "tour" and a demonstration of how the system worked. For the next of couple hours, Michelle was unflappable. She answered questions about how the software and hardware interacted to create a new call center experience for restaurant operators. She spouted facts, figures, statistics, technical information— you name it. She hit every ball out of the park.

But what those executives didn't know about Michelle is that only a few years ago she considered herself physically handicapped and mentally slow. I have the video to prove it— and the next morning I showed it to these McDonald's guys. You see, Michelle didn't work her way up through my company because she was the most talented or best educated. She worked hard every day to provide for her family and is still driven by

81

that passion. A victim of rape and domestic abuse, Michelle has always had to fend for herself and take care of her two kids at all costs. In the interview from years back, Michelle is hunched as she talks humbly about the prospect of one day owning a computer, having a reliable car and living in an apartment with a bathtub in it. This woman never thought in just a few short years she'd be running a call center and sitting right outside my office every day. In fact, she had decided she wants to have her own call center one day. She didn't let her circumstances talk her into laziness—or worse, a victim mentality. She got up off her ass and did something. Today, she works for Checks Unlimited, one of the largest personal check companies in the US She's moving up, and I believe she's one step closer to fulfilling her dream.

Michelle had every reason not to get up. Life had kicked her down, hard. But she did, and she used her gifts. She couldn't do it alone. Michelle needed to leverage other people, her "team," to help her accomplish her goals.

Collaboration and Teamwork

To borrow from Thomas Friedman, the "flat world" has made collaboration and teamwork much easier. *The World is Flat* is full of stories about collaboration and teamwork made possible only by the extraordinary technological advances of the 1990s. In fact, on page 40, you can read about "Flat Burgers and Fries," which talks about the call center where Michelle worked. I suspect that people's fascination with collaboration comes from the economic realities forcing us all to do more with less. Collaboration is seen as a way to boost productivity through more efficient working relationships. It's a powerful paradigm, and it's really too bad that most people hopelessly mess up collaboration. When you understand the essential nature of collaboration and teamwork, you might find it's a lot different from your current opinion. What do you think it is? Write up a quick definition, and later we'll compare notes.

My definition of **collaboration** is the process of identifying resources *outside* of your organization that you need to create a more efficient result for your customers. The potential for collaboration exists inside any group of people— it's not limited to businesses. The principle here is that someone else has something you need to improve your productivity.

Teamwork is the process of working together with other people to achieve a common goal. It's not limited to businesses—we need teamwork to accomplish most things in life.

There's a story in *The World is Flat* that reflects the kind of collaboration I'm talking about. Although I am profiled in the book, I thought I'd highlight two other great companies: UPS and Toshiba. Friedman explains how Toshiba was able to significantly improve turnaround time for laptop repairs by partnering with shipping giant UPS. Now, with only that as an introduction, you might think that the two companies came up with some great pricing structure to get the computers to and from Toshiba with greater speed. That's a reasonable hypothesis. If Toshiba gets the computers faster, it can repair and ship them back more quickly.

Instead of simply speeding up the shipments, Toshiba and UPS came up with a brilliant strategy. UPS agreed, as part of its contract with Toshiba, to train laptop repair specialists who would work from UPS's domestic hub in Louisville, Kentucky. These new employees work for UPS, but are trained by Toshiba to repair computers to their company standards. It's more efficient for UPS to receive all Toshiba computers at their hub, and much easier—and quicker—to repair them there and immediately ship them back out to the customer. It cut days off of their turnaround time and resulted in thousands of happy customers who didn't have to live without their laptops for several more days.

My interpretation is pretty simple: **Sometimes two different problems share a common solution.** Toshiba and UPS don't have much in common, and their problems were very different. However, the common solution met the needs of each company in exactly the right way. Toshiba was looking for ways to speed up laptop repair for customers so it could cut costs and boost productivity. On the other side, UPS needed to find ways to compete against FedEx for market share— especially on big lucrative contracts. UPS executives knew that trying to out-ship FedEx probably wouldn't work, so, instead, they developed a completely new idea to create a whole new income stream. Now we have two companies with one solution that meets the needs of both. UPS gets the contract with a new model for its business-to-business commerce. Toshiba reaps the benefits of efficiently shipping packages to one central location for repair. Collaboration often means finding one solution that solves multiple problems.

Now, let's look at teamwork. In order for UPS and Toshiba to execute this plan, they needed a high degree of teamwork. UPS proposed that Toshiba outsource a major function, laptop repair, to a company best known for delivering packages. In order for this to work, both teams needed to work together in pursuit of their common goal. Andrew Carnegie, the great American industrialist and philanthropist, likened teamwork to fuel. Teamwork is never the end result; it is a resource to drive you toward your ultimate result. LA Lakers coach Phil Jackson has coached incredible teams that have won many NBA

84

championships. But no one would care about them if they didn't win that ultimate prize! Having a great team doesn't mean much if you cannot convert that fuel into results. In the UPS/Toshiba example, neither company could afford to confuse building a good team with attaining the proper result. Getting to your result effectively means putting some real brain time into the following:

1) Define the need and explore every available avenue to meet that end. Use the "The Whys" Drill exercise from Chapter 1 to make sure you really understand all the aspects and options associated with your task or project.

2) Establish the best people for the team. Do you think Toshiba trained truck drivers to repair their computers? Of course not. Managers knew they needed trained IT repair staff and created their job descriptions accordingly.

3) Determine what success means, and convey that vision to everyone on your team. You've gotta know. In this case, success for Toshiba means faster turnaround of repairs and happier customers.

4) Ask yourself if you're absolutely committed to the team's success. If any part of you answers no, you need to abort the mission. Teams do not work when the coach is not *passionately* invested in winning every game.

BIGG IDEA: ALWAYS CONSIDER THE QUESTION "WHAT'S IN IT FOR ME?"

What's in it for Me?

Sounds like a pretty selfish conclusion for such a team-oriented chapter. But the bottom line to collaboration is that it works best when the people involved pursue their vested self-interests. What's in it for the credit union when it lends to a low-wage earner who just opened her first-ever bank account? Lots of things: good press, compliance with the Federal Community Reinvestment Act, and return on the mission that is established by their charter to help poorer communities. Did you know that about financial institutions? It's one of their jobs to help low-income families. Finally, they earn customers for life! When you help someone become self-sufficient, he or she becomes very loyal to you.

I can get anyone to join something, but he is never going to put his heart into it unless there is something in it for him. For this reason, any collaboration you are involved in must answer the question: **What's in it for me?** In the America's Family example:

- The employer gets help in persuading employees to come to work. Employees stay longer and are more loyal and productive.
- The employees get the benefits they need to be successful at their jobs and stay out of life's emergency room. They eventually graduate to a better life.
- The nonprofit organizations and public agencies get a more efficient way to deliver their goods and service
- The for-profit companies get access to people who wouldn't otherwise be buying their goods and services.

86

Everybody wins. Teamwork and collaboration are powerful tools to achieve things you cannot reach on your own, but the whole concept revolves around the question "What's in it for me?"

You'll find that you can even exceed your goals when you've got people on your team who are committed to a corporate vision that reflects their individual interests.

Chapter 8

Serving Your Guts Out

People are illogical, unreasonable, and self-centered.
Love them anyway.

If you do good, people will accuse you of
selfish ulterior motives.
Do good anyway.

If you are successful, you will win false
friends and true enemies.
Succeed anyway.

The good you do today will be forgotten tomorrow.
Do good anyway.

Honesty and frankness make you vulnerable.
Be honest and frank anyway.

The biggest men and women with the biggest ideas can
be shot down by the smallest men and
women with the smallest minds.
Think big anyway.

People favor underdogs but follow only top dogs.
Fight for a few underdogs anyway.

What you spend years building may be
destroyed overnight.
Build anyway.

People really need help but may attack
you if you do help them.
Help people anyway.

Give the world the best you have and
you'll get kicked in the teeth.
Give the world the best you have anyway.

Dr. Kent Keith

God Blessed the Broken Road...

Kent Keith wrote the "Paradoxical Commandments" when he was a 19-year-old sophomore at Harvard University in 1968. Since that time, they have been used by millions of people. Even Mother Teresa posted a version in a children's home in Calcutta where the Sisters of Charity ministered to the poor and downtrodden. The essence of servant leadership is found in these "commandments." My BIGG IDEA, in the tradition of these commandments, is:

**BIGG IDEA: YOU WILL NEVER HAVE ALL
YOUR NEEDS COMPLETELY MET. MEET
THE NEEDS OF OTHERS ANYWAY.**

After I was divorced, I vowed never to marry again. Ask my kids: They'll tell you I was a confirmed bachelor. That is, until

Brenda stole my heart. Brenda worked for me at Bigari Foods, and I knew her for a couple of years before we started dating. One night, I was out to dinner with my two older daughters, Sara and Cali. During the course of dinner, Sara asked me, "Dad, when are you going to ask Brenda to marry you?"

"Baby," I replied to my precious first-born daughter, "see that light socket over there? Go stick your finger in it."

"What?" she said, giving me a puzzled look.

"When you come back to the table, I'm going to send you back over there and tell you to do it again. That's when I'm going to ask Brenda to marry me," I responded.

The girls knew that Brenda was the best thing that had happened to our family, but I wasn't listening. But I did start thinking. At about the same time, Joe Johnson, my director of operations, told me he wanted to buy my house. He said, "Well, since you and Brenda are going to get married and buy a new house, I thought I'd buy the one you're living in now." It was like a coordinated attack on my bachelorhood. I thought some more. A couple of months later, I asked Brenda to marry me.

While we were dating, Brenda was in the process of adopting a daughter from China. Brenda was also divorced. She wasn't able to give birth to a child, and she really didn't know if she'd ever have a husband again. But one thing was clear to her: She was made for being a mom and raising a child. So, with few resources, Brenda started the expensive, year-long adoption process. I was her boss. I knew what her salary was. In order to get this done, she went through significant financial sacrifice— which included buying a 900 square-foot house with a back yard for her child. We called it the "Barbie House." It wasn't a requirement for the adoption, but she knew in her heart it was the right thing to do. She saved up and paid all the money

91

on her own, and by the time we were dating, she was right in the middle of adopting Anna Mei from China. It was one of the things that really drew me to her. She had decided she was going to be a servant. Brenda will tell you that she believed God had selected a child for her somewhere in the world; she just had to go search and find that baby.

Here I am, a guy with tremendous financial resources, and I had never considered adopting a child. Never! I never wanted to be a father of young kids while I was in my forties. Forget it! But once Brenda returned from China with Anna Mei, I fell in love with mother and child. Because of her example, I wanted to serve them! I fell in love watching Brenda's servant heart and the selfless way she put aside everything in her life for a kid she'd never met. It's just like the Rascal Flatts song lyrics: "God blessed the broken road that led me straight to you."[20]

It wasn't always easy, but I wouldn't trade the outcome for anything. I had my doubts, too. My biggest fear, other than getting married again, was that I wouldn't love Anna as much as I loved my two biological daughters, Sara and Cali. But Anna immediately stole my heart, and I don't see an adopted Chinese girl anymore. I just see Anna Mei Bigari—my own flesh and blood. Brenda and I went on to adopt Matthew and Zachary, so we now have three kids under the age of five. The only way this can happen, in my opinion, is by putting your own needs aside to meet the needs of others. It defies logic and explanation. No rational person would do it. But it works. That's what servant leadership, and the rest of this chapter, is really about.

Servant Leadership

Servant leadership, like Brenda practiced when she adopted Anna, is the most effective leadership style available to you today. You may be familiar with this concept, or even know some people who you think are good examples of this principle. I think it's helpful to contrast servant leadership with its opposite—autocratic leadership. An autocrat is a person who rules with absolute or unlimited power without regard to others. Autocratic leaders believe that most employees are generally lazy, need constant supervision and are only motivated by fear-inducing threats and management crackdowns. You might know them by other names: micromanagers, tyrants, bullies, despots…you fill in the blank.

It's important to note that not all of these leaders are bad. In some cases, autocratic leadership is all they know how to practice. It is comfortable for many Type-A, concrete thinkers to organize things into hierarchies. What is dangerous about the autocratic leader is the potential for stifling the creativity, passion and excellence in others. When the autocrat knows it all, everyone else becomes slave or servant.

With servant leadership, you are dealing with a completely different approach to working relationships. The term "servant leadership" is relatively new. In 1970, Robert Greenleaf wrote an essay titled *The Servant as Leader* that introduced the world to his groundbreaking research and ideas. For decades, Greenleaf had studied how large companies used authoritarian and hierarchical models of management. His observations indicated that power-centered leadership was no longer working, and new models were needed. In *The Servant as Leader*, Greenleaf coined the term "servant leadership," and described it as the process whereby leaders choose to serve first, and then out of service comes the conscious choice to lead. He contrasts that with the "leader-first" personality, who puts wealth, possessions and power first, and then chooses to serve.

93

Others, like Stephen Covey, Peter Senge, and Ken Blanchard, have greatly expanded on Greenleaf's original ideas in their books about life and effective leadership. In practice, servant leadership positions the leader as a steward of various resources who is responsible for the proper development and growth of those resources. Whether those resources are human beings, factories or flowers, the servant leader applies influence by caring for those resources in a way that improves productivity and the bottom line.

Greenleaf makes it clear that the servant leader chooses to serve first and then to lead because he or she wants to become a better servant. At the root of this paradigm is the deeply held belief that service to others is the most effective and efficient way to achieve organizational results. I know I must sound a little mushy for a West Point military man. But this is where servant leadership gets a bad rap. Being a servant does not mean you never use authority, give orders or set expectations. My father did those things all the time, yet he maintained his posture as a servant leader. Servant leaders are still leaders of others. The key difference is in the *choice* to pursue results by serving others first.

Serving Your Guts Out

No matter where you are in your life, you can become a servant leader. People say, "This is a great idea, but it will never work in the real world." You know, it always works, and here are ways you can cultivate these principles in your own life.

1) Put yourself second.

The most important thing is to leave your fear behind. One of the fears in servant-based leadership is that by putting

94

yourself second, you'll become weaker. I once asked an NFL sports agent why the Green Bay Packers hired Mike McCarthy as their head coach when he had a paltry 4-12 record as the offensive coordinator of the San Francisco 49ers. The agent observed that a great coach could threaten the job security of team executives. So they brought in someone who doesn't represent a threat to the GM.

If you're skeptical, consider that about one-third of NFL football teams hired new coaches this year, and most of them had less-than-stellar records.

2) Embrace talented people.

Most leaders are afraid that younger and more talented people will overtake them and put them out of their jobs. As a leader, you want to surround yourself with smart people and inspire them with a vision for the future. There's no sense in fearing smart and talented people. Instead, let them achieve your vision. From my perspective, technically, they can do the job better than I can! But that's the whole point. When they succeed, you are freed up to step back into a strategic visionary role, allowing others to implement the plan and quickly rise to prominence and great success. Your job is to cast the vision— that is the strategic approach to leadership. Tactically speaking, your team should be able to do it better than you. If they can't, you've got the wrong team. It's a win-win scenario here.

3) Be a barrier basher.

Servant-based leaders remove barriers to other people's success. I spend a good portion of my day kicking down obstacles that are holding back the people who work for me. This creates a healthy working relationship and an opportunity for lots of teachable moments. People in my companies know that I am concerned only about things that are important. This allows people to engage me when they know they are up against a barrier in an important project and I am the only one who can help them through it. It also gives me the opportunity to show people the difference between something important and something trivial.

4)   Find teachable moments.

There is an exercise I used to take my McDonald's managers through to teach them how to handle customer complaints. In the fast-food business, you get a lot of interesting customers. My favorites are the elderly retired folk who think that my restaurant is their personal store for sugar packets, coffee creamer and napkins. And of course, it's always these customers who complain most loudly when something doesn't go right. We watched one guy steal a bunch of napkins and sugar packets. The next day he came back to complain that the drive-thru forgot to give him a fork with his salad. I wanted to teach my managers how to handle complaints like this, so I took about $200 in tens, twenties, and fifties and mixed them up with some of the day's worst garbage. I brought that bag of trash into the manager's meeting and dumped the contents onto the table. Imagine a nice conference room table covered in every kind of fast-food filth you can think of—coffee, soda, ketchup, and "special sauce." It was a sticky, disgusting mess. My managers looked at me like I was crazy. Then, one of them saw a ten-dollar bill wedged in some old French fries. "Look what I found," he yelled. Pretty soon, the managers started rifling through the garbage, looking for the cash. "It's the same way with customers," I tell them. "You have to handle each customer's complaint as if you were looking for a $20 bill on a table full of garbage. There's a pearl in what they're telling you; you've just got to sift through garbage to get to it." In the case of the sugar-stealing senior citizen with no salad fork, it helped drive a systematic solution. We apologized and gave him a coupon for a free salad (because we knew he liked free stuff). Then we implemented a system of taping the fork to the top of the salad box. That was the pearl.

5) Impart vision through storytelling.

People learn best through stories. Think about your own life. Recall the greatest teachers you've ever had, and think about what they did differently. My hunch is that they illustrated their lessons with great stories and used every opportunity to **show** you the lesson, rather than just teach you about it. That's one reason why this book is full of stories. You have to dig out lots of the gems. I don't give you the answers because I don't have them. Instead, I've got a bunch of goofy parables about throwing BBQ sauce and dumping garbage on the table. What can you get out of that? Once you read it through your specific context, I think there's a lot to glean here. The point is, people learn from stories. People who have the desire to learn, are able to take the story, personalize it and adapt it to their situation.

6) Delegate principles, not tasks.

When you put these principles to work, it creates a win-win situation for you and your team. In my context, when an individual invests in a short-term relationship with me, my job is to help them move on to bigger and better things, while at the same time helping me to become more successful. I don't want them to stay with the organization forever. I want them to grow into better roles somewhere else. I will teach them strategic, servant-based living that says, "I'm going to cast a big vision for you. When you take this vision as a student, you'll exceed the teacher." That's always the goal. Depending on where you are in life, you either want to rise as far as you can and then go on to something bigger, or you want to help someone younger and less experienced to do the same. Ideally, you'll accomplish both at the same time.

In every aspect of life, this strategy really reflects the BIGG IDEA: **Vision attracts talent.** Think of it this way: When you cultivate a reputation for building solid leaders and then setting them free to succeed in other ventures, you are putting out a big signpost that says, "We value you! Come here and let us teach you all that we know so that together we can be more successful than you ever imagined." What a great reputation to have! Anyone—a business leader, parent or volunteer—can help build others up through servant-based living. But the vision cannot be strictly self-serving. There must be something in it that creates a win-win scenario for both you and the members on your team. When you achieve this, you'll see that you've actually put yourself second, and you're using your vision to serve the leaders you've gathered around you. Remember that the greatest servant leaders put others first, embrace talent, remove obstacles, find teachable moments and tell lots of stories.

Practical Exercise

In order to really get this principle, you have to experiment. My hypothesis is this: *If you employ these servant-based leadership strategies, then you will build exemplary leaders around you.* In order to test this idea, find the most difficult person in your life. Then follow these instructions:

1) Put this person first in your relationship. Write out tangible ways you can do this. Ask the person about the barriers and

obstacles in his or her life that you can push down for them. Have some of your own ideas ready before you talk to them.

2) Develop one "teachable moment" for you and this person. Write out what you are going to do.

3) Write a story to share key leadership concepts with this person.

Now, here's the great part: If you try this with the most difficult person in your life and it works, think of what will happen if all your relationships follow this pattern!

However, it's my sincere belief that if you intentionally pursue a strategy of servant-based leadership and it fails, then it is more about the other person than you. If it's a relationship you can end, that would be my advice. If it's your mother-in-law…well, you're on your own with that one.

Following the lead of Mother Teresa (who was a shining example of servant leadership), print out Dr. Keith's commandments and post them where you'll see them the most. You may not have to travel across the globe, as Brenda did, to find your opportunity to live these commandments. But stay open each day for possibilities to invest in others. The return will surpass any financial gain you could ever imagine, for you and the people who cross your path.

Chapter 9

This is Not a Frat

It is no use saying, "We are doing our best."
You have got to succeed in doing
what is necessary.

Winston Churchill

Two years into my education at West Point, I made the decision that it was time for me to move on. You see, I was a sophomore, a football player, in the top 10 percent of the class and a pretty big deal. What bothered me was that I wasn't really getting enough attention. I was feeling a little sorry for myself, and I felt that a major decision was looming on the horizon. You can freely leave West Point before the start of your junior year. But after crossing that threshold, you're contractually committed to the Army. Drop out after that point, and you're automatically enlisted. At that time, I was feeling underappreciated—after all, I was a great asset to that venerable organization. So I made an appointment with my tactical officer, Maj. Weller, to talk about how I was feeling. I knew that Maj. Weller thought the world of me and understood how important I was to the Army. He'd never let me quit.

I walked into his office (the door was always open) and saluted my superior officer.

"Hey, Bigari, good to see you, how have you been? Have a seat. What can I do for you today?" he said as I stood in front of his desk.

"Well, sir," I started, "I'm thinking about quitting. I'm wondering if we might discuss that?"

I'd had dozens of conversations with Maj. Weller, and he was always engaged and treated me with respect. I had always known him as the consummate military professional, so I expected the same treatment in this situation. I wanted him to talk me out of quitting—to coddle me, tell me how important I was. Deep down, that's what I was looking for from Maj. Weller.

I'll never forget his response. He opened up his Army-issue desk and pulled out a file from one of the drawers. He took out some forms, spread them on the desk in front of me and said, "Son, sign here, here, and here, and I'll have your ass out of here in 72 hours." Each stab of his finger on the forms was like a thunderclap.

"But, sir!" I said. "I just wanted to discuss it." My head was still ringing from Maj. Weller's abrupt treatment. Surely he was going to fight for me to stay. Me, Steve Bigari, the Army's most valuable soldier!

He just wagged his finger at me. "No son," he said, "you don't understand. This is not a frat. Here, you're 100 percent in or you're 100 percent gone. So, do you want to sign the papers?"

Stunned, I stammered, "Uh, no sir...I think I'm okay. Thank you." I saluted, turned and left the room. In all my organizations since then, this incident has stuck in my mind.

When I was at Brown University, I rushed Delta Tau Delta. I ran naked around the quad. I set couches on fire, threw them out of windows and then peed on them from the second story of the frat house. And the difference between a frat and an excellent organization is simple. A frat is a place where relationship transcends everything. Everything is about bonding with your "brothers," mostly through disgusting and near-criminal behavior. But in a world-class organization, the relationships are based on performance. Without performance, there is nothing. You can have wonderful relationships, but the foundation of those relationships is what you do, how you behave, and whom you can count on. That makes the relationships better, deeper, richer.

BIGG IDEA: LIFE IS NOT A FRAT. YOU'RE EITHER 100 PERCENT IN, OR 100 PERCENT OUT.

Even in your family life, relationships are based on a foundation of performance. I can't think of a relationship worth having that is not dependent upon some kind of performance. In your family, that foundation is self-denial—or at least I believe it should be.

What about you? Is your family some kind of low-grade chicken outfit to you? Are your kids spoiled brats? Is your spouse a deadbeat? If you're passionate about your work or fantasy football, shouldn't you be passionate about your family, too? Really, the approach to building a great organization isn't, fundamentally, that different from building a strong family. There are plenty of families out there that don't give a rip about each other or what happens inside their four walls, and they're chicken outfits—not something you'd want to be a part of.

Great families, like great organizations, are based on investment, loyalty and performance. I have a friend who gets up every morning and makes his wife a caramel latte. He's not a perfect husband, but every day he is committed to that act of service. It's a small reflection of his greater commitment. I know there are hundreds of things that they both do—for each other, their kids, and their lives together—that make their family the opposite of a chicken outfit. When Maj. Weller said, "This is not a frat," he meant that you are either passionately committed or you are passionately *not* committed. No middle ground. The same is true for any organization or family. The family that lives out this model experiences something that is better, deeper and richer.

Some people, at home or at the office, believe that close relationships give us license to excuse incompetence or sub-par performance. Have you ever been in a situation in which a friend asks you to cover for a mistake he's made? It happens all the time. Over time, it develops into a "good enough" attitude. We expect standards to be lower for good friends or people in similar circumstances. What a bunch of crap.

In my relationships, all the standards are higher because the foundations of trust run deeper. A good relationship gives you the ability to build a solid set of performance expectations. It also comes with a buffer zone that allows for shortcomings. Call it equity.

Now, don't waste your equity on something like personal favors. You're going to make mistakes, and others will too. People get that. I'm not saying that the relationships with people you work with are the same as those in your personal life. I care about the people I work with, but I'd throw myself in front of an 18-wheeler for Brenda. She knows my level of commitment and trusts it. So when I make mistakes—and I do—our relationship is not in trouble. Where you run into danger, at work or home, is when the relationship lacks that foundation of commitment, when there's zero equity.

I'm a strong believer in having favored relationships in the workplace. In fact, it's pretty easy to see that those relationships with a good foundation and lots of trust will be favored. That's okay. But you should follow a few guidelines. If you're anything like me, you have an inner circle of people with whom you work closely with on a daily basis. Let's face it, the people in this inner circle are favored. However, within the circle, there are no favorites. In reality, you can't feel equally about every person, but if others in the inner circle can tell who the favorites are, you've got a problem.

One of the ways you show favoritism is through spending time with people. If you want to improve a relationship, it is almost a guarantee that if you devote more time to it, it will grow accordingly. Of course, this must unfold within strict boundaries, but anything you devote time to will grow. Time is your most precious commodity. Make sure people know that, so that when they do get some of it, they understand how valuable it really is.

Maj. Weller had spent time with me—we respected each other and had built trust. But when my level of commitment was in question, he wasted no time in letting me know my options.

What Does It Mean for You?
1)   Every relationship in your life has a purpose and a mission.

That may have a mercenary ring, but it is very true. My relationship with Jennifer Chandler at America's Family is about helping 39 million hard-working Americans find the resources to attain true prosperity. In my family, our mission is to honor God, each other and our kids. With Joe Johnson, my purpose in his life was to leverage my resources to help catapult him into restaurant ownership.

105

2) Relationships need deep foundations.

You can't take time to build deep foundations in every relationship, but every one of your significant relationships needs one. What does that look like? I'll give you a few examples.

One of my kids' favorite movies is *Ice Age*. In case you haven't seen it, it's about a motley crew of prehistoric animals—a woolly mammoth, a saber-toothed tiger, and an annoying rodent with buck teeth—who are traveling a long distance to safety. Throughout the movie, the characters say, "The herd has to stay together, because that's what herds do!" That foundation is based on a natural instinct. In the human arena, this would be culture. Marriage vows, a contract, a common passion, a quest for survival— these are some of the elements that make a solid foundation.

3) Great relationships have equity.

Good relationships have a foundation. Great relationships turn those cultural or legal foundations into something far deeper. For example, Joe Johnson is a partner in one of my businesses. The only reason he's a partner is because of the deep foundation we've built as co-workers over the past ten years. The fact that I've known him for ten years isn't the big deal. What is important is his consistent performance over a decade of working together. I could have said, "Hey, Joe's worked here for ten years; he deserves to be a partner." But that's kind of insulting. Instead, Joe is brought into a circle of trust because of his performance and the foundation that performance has built over time. That's called equity.

Practical Exercise

Think of a relationship in your life that is truly worthwhile to you and begin to put it through the grid below.

On one page, I want you to write the story of your relationship with one other human being by using the following "starters." If you're really creative, you can use your own. These are designed to help you think about how relationships work together.

The purpose of this relationship is…

Write a mission statement for this relationship. I already told you about Brenda and me. Think about the ultimate purpose of the relationship and describe it in specific words. Missions focus on what you are doing today—not what you want to become in the future. Make it action-oriented and present tense.

The foundation of this relationship is…

You first might describe the technical details of this relationship. Is it culturally based, legally defined or undefined? Also, picture in your mind the foundation as a real thing. Is it broad or narrow? Is it shallow or deep? Is it structurally sound or does it need repair? Think about the foundation of your relationship like a real building foundation, and then describe it based on the picture in your mind.

The equity level in this relationship is…

There are couple of ways you can answer this one. Would you take a bullet for this person? Would he throw you under the bus to make himself look good? Maybe you'd do that to him. You should stress-test your relationship by dreaming up scenarios and watching your response to them. If you find yourself with an abundance of grace and empathy—even in the worst of situations—then you've got lots of equity. However, if you find yourself short-tempered or quickly annoyed, you're probably looking at a poor relationship.

I can change this relationship for the better by . . .

You can change only yourself. This is a hard lesson for most people to learn, but changing other people is beyond your capabilities. Ask any woman who's ever tried to change a man, and she'll tell you—it had to be his idea. When you evaluate relationships, you've got to focus on the only thing you can control: your own behavior. That doesn't mean you can't talk to someone in a constructive way about a negative trait or behavior—just remember, it's only a request.

I honor this relationship when I . . .

Honor is not a familiar concept in Western societies because our roots are in law-based European cultures. However, many cultures have honor-based codes of conduct. These are largely unwritten laws that dictate how individuals interact with one another. In these cultures, it is desirable to pursue honorable behavior regardless of the prevailing laws.

Allow me to steal an example from Gary Smalley. Smalley is a marriage and family expert who gives seminars all over the country. When he talks about honor, he brings out a 400-year-old, $2 million Stradivarius violin. Once he announces this, everyone wants to see it up close. Now, imagine that the person in this relationship is the valuable violin, and write down how you would treat him or her differently. To truly honor someone means going beyond the bounds of what your legal relationship calls for to pursue a much higher standard. What do you want that standard to be?

You should now have a one-page write-up about this relationship. So what now? What are you going to do with this information? Ultimately, that's up to you. I believe you should write a short action plan that provides specific details about how you will build a better relationship with the person you wrote about. Better still, get off your ass and share it with them! You thought enough of the relationship to write about it—now honor this person by making yourself vulnerable. Neither of you will ever forget the conversation.

Chapter 10

You Can't Take "No"
for an Answer

*Change does not roll in on the wheels of inevitability, but comes
through continuous struggle. And so we must straighten our backs and
work for our freedom. A man can't ride you unless your back is bent.*

Martin Luther King, Jr.

When I was in the Army, I was stationed at Fort Carson
in Colorado Springs. I quickly rose through the ranks to platoon
leader and eventually became executive officer of one of the best
engineering companies in the entire US Army. Because of these
accomplishments, I was promoted to adjutant, the personnel
officer who is in charge of awards, recognition, discipline and
any other duties performed in a normal personnel department.
This battalion was run by an Army colonel and as the adjutant,
I was his aide. My desk was immediately outside the colonel's
office, where I handled the scheduling and problem-solving for
our entire battalion. Basically, I managed everything in his life.
My first assignment was with Col. Tom Farewell, but he was only
in the job a few months before he was replaced by a guy named
Dick Johns. Before taking the post, the colonels conspired to
keep me as the adjutant for the battalion. They thought I could
be talked into staying in the Army for life. That was their plan
anyway.

So Col. Johns hit Fort Carson. He was an unconventional guy with a unique and dynamic leadership style. He routinely had an unlit cigar hanging out of his mouth. Johns was referred to as "The Skull," a nickname used by the infantry and armor officers from a previous assignment because of his leadership style—and the fact that he was essentially bald. The Skull intimidated most people on post, but I loved him. He said things like, "Biggs, 'no' is just where the negotiation starts," or "Biggs, you can't take 'no' for an answer," or "Why are you even telling me this? Figure out a way around it!" He just pounded it into my head. It didn't matter who was saying "no." Even if it was a general, The Skull expected me to find a way around it. And I got pretty good at it. It wasn't always the direct path or the conventional way, but I would figure out how to get the job done.

One day, my brother-in-law and his girlfriend were visiting on the day of a live-fire hand grenade exercise that one of the lieutenants in the unit was running. I thought it would be really fun to take them out to see a cool military operation. I got a little too excited. The way my mind works, I try to make things bigger and better. Somehow, I came up with the great idea of letting these two civilians participate in the exercise and throw a hand grenade themselves.

"Man," I thought, "they would think it's really cool to throw a live hand grenade!" I figured I better not do this without permission from The Skull. I walked into his office and he said, "What can I do for you, Biggs?"

"Well sir, I was wondering something, hypothetically. If somebody's brother-in-law were to come out and visit, what would you think about asking permission, hypothetically, for taking him out on the live-fire hand grenade range to throw hand grenades? Hypothetically, sir."

The Skull took the unlit cigar from his mouth. Without lifting his head to look at me he simply said, "I think somebody who would ask that would be an idiot for asking." He put the cigar back in his mouth and continued working. Somehow in this exchange, I believed that I had received permission from The Skull to endanger the lives of two civilians at a live-fire hand grenade exercise.

We headed down to the range where the exercise was under way, which caused a stir in itself, because, well, it's very rare to see civilians around live hand grenades. After pulling up in my jeep, I explained to the lieutenant in charge what my plan was and offered to relieve him of duty so he wouldn't get into any trouble. As the safety officer, he could get court-martialed if anything went wrong—like two civilians getting blown up during his training exercise.

"Sounds good to me," was the lieutenant's response, and we proceeded down to one of the bunkers where one of my top guys, Sgt. 1st Class Pernia, was getting the next batch of grenades ready. These grenade bunkers are just three cinderblock walls about four feet high. It's a pretty simple exercise. You grab the grenade, pull out the pin—just like in the movies—and throw it in the direction you want it to explode. The pin holds the "spoon" in place, and once that spoon falls away from the grenade, you have about three to five seconds before detonation. Until you let go, you can always put the pin back in. But once the spoon is detached, the grenade will go off. No two grenades are the same—some explode in three seconds, others in seven. You can imagine that timing is absolutely critical.

My brother-in-law was up first. Sgt. Pernia gave him a quick tutorial and then handed him a live grenade. From my vantage point, I could tell he was shaking pretty badly. It was, after all, a live grenade. He pulled the pin, lobbed the grenade over the wall of the bunker, and put his head down like Pernia taught him. BOOM! The grenade exploded in the distance and everybody started cheering. Next up, the girlfriend. Now I could tell she was shaking before she even stepped foot in the bunker. Pernia grabbed the grenade and put it into her very shaky hands. Slowly, she pulled the pin from the grenade and made a move like she was going to throw it—but something didn't look quite right.

CLANG!

She dropped the grenade on the floor of the bunker. The spoon clattered off in one direction while the grenade bounced on the concrete a couple times.

The next few seconds played out in slow motion through my mind's eye. I saw bodies, exploded onto the concrete walls of the bunker. Medical teams scraping up remains with shovels. Shrapnel from the grenade injuring me. And I saw myself, court-martialed and spending the rest of my life in an Army prison, riddled with guilt. I'd just pissed my career down the drain, not to mention possibly killing family, coworkers, and friends.

Worst of all, I'd have to face The Skull.

Then, out of nowhere, Pernia scooped up the grenade with one hand, threw it over the wall and slammed the girlfriend to the floor, covering her with his body.

BOOM!

The grenade exploded about a foot from the bunker's front wall.

"I think we're done now," I announced. We hopped into the jeep and rode back to my office.

What Does This Mean to You?

My grenade story is obviously about extremes, which brings us back to the concept of boundaries. Not taking "no" for an answer doesn't mean you should violate ethical (or sensible) boundaries. I took two untrained civilians and put them in a live-fire combat situation. That's not cool—it was incredibly irresponsible of me. I'm lucky that no one was hurt or killed by that stunt, because I never would've been able to live with that. You can't ignore the legal and ethical boundaries in the name of "not taking 'no' for an answer." I learned this the hard way by almost blowing someone up. Don't steal that idea, okay?

Here's an example from my time with The Skull that illustrates this principle. The roots of our battalion extended all the way back to the Civil War. Over those many years, tens of thousands of men and women from our unit had died in the service of our country. Each year, the engineering unit would celebrate and commemorate those accomplishments at an annual banquet. This year, The Skull wanted to buy a sterling-silver punch bowl and have it engraved with the names of those in the unit. This was a very expensive proposition, but The Skull wanted it. The Army had no money, but The Skull would not take "no" for an answer. When I asked The Skull how we were going to pay for it, he said, "You know what I think, Biggs?"

"No, sir. What's that?" I replied, nervous about what he would say.

"So many people have bled for this punch bowl, I think we should bleed for this punch bowl too!" he exclaimed.

The Skull's idea was to have everyone in the unit raise money through plasmapheresis—selling blood platelets to companies who use it to make cosmetics and other products. The soldiers were paid $16.00 per visit. I was willing to give blood

115

(to a hospital), but not to sell it (to a profit-making company). To resolve my moral qualms, I decided I to give my blood to the hospital and donate my own $16.00 each time to the unit's fund-raising effort. That's the only way I could reconcile it in my mind. The Skull wasn't going to take "no" for an answer, which meant I had to bleed for the damn punch bowl!

The punch bowl is still at Fort Carson today, and when I tell my Army buddies about how we bled for it, they crack up. You see, The Skull was going to get the punch bowl one way or another. In his mind, it made perfect sense to have everyone raise money by selling blood. I couldn't tell him no, so I had to come up with a creative way around it to accomplish the same goal.

I had seen The Skull do this so many times and in such a masterful way, that eventually I realized that "no" is just where the negotiation begins. In life, too many people accept "no" for an answer. "Sorry," they tell me, "I tried my best but they told me 'no.' What do you want me to do?" Here's what I say:

BIGG IDEA: DON'T TAKE "NO" FOR AN ANSWER— FIGURE OUT HOW TO GET AROUND, PAST OR THROUGH THE OBJECTION.

Don't go back to your boss for solutions. Wise people seek alternate ways to get a job done even in the face of opposition, dissent or nay-saying. Whatever you're faced with, there is a solution. Through wit, charm and perseverance, you don't have to take "no" for an answer.

In my own career, I've employed this tactic many times. There's a wonderful book on negotiation called *Getting to Yes: Negotiating Agreement Without Giving In* written by two geniuses from the Harvard Business School, Roger Fisher and William Ury. According to the book, getting to "yes" requires finding the right path. Sometimes it's easy. But most days, you've got to climb, dig, crawl, sprint, dance and shimmy your way to "yes." You can get there, but it is rarely easy. Don't expect it to come directly, on a silver platter (or in a silver punch bowl, either).

One very successful way to do this is to look for the common thread or shared interests between you and the individual you are disagreeing with. You want to help them answer the question, "What's in it for me?" This is very standard negotiation stuff, and there are tons of books on the subject. The difference between me and the negotiation guys is just politeness. Most people do take "no" for an answer because it's the polite thing to do. In my world, I'm just wearing down the guy across the table by coming up with option after option for him to consider. Eventually, I find a bridge. Think about the movie *Forrest Gump*. Tom Hanks' character just doesn't know how to take "no" for an answer. In his mind, he and Jenny go together like "peas and carrots." He never, ever loses sight of that and continues to find ways to connect with Jenny, find common ground and express his love.[21]

Here's another great example from the movies. Remember *Dumb and Dumber*? At the very end of the movie, Jim Carrey's character asks Lauren Holley if they'll ever end up together. After she quotes him the impossible odds, Carrey says, "So there's a chance!"[22]

Goofy as they are, both are examples about not taking "no" for an answer. Just keep trying, despite the odds. Eventually you'll score the option that works.

Now, in all of your persistence, you can't throw out the legal and ethical boundaries. Some are quick to do this—even in small ways. Look no further than the dramatic rise in white-collar crime over the past ten years. You can't cook the books just to meet your quarterly earnings estimates. Find another way, because that one is out of bounds. These ethical lapses happen too frequently, and you can never become a person of integrity if you are willing to put aside your ethical convictions just to make a buck or get your way. I've made poor decisions in the past, like giving people in my family live hand grenades, and they never turn out the way you want them to. Anything that is legal, moral and ethical is in bounds. Resist the temptation and danger that comes from a quick but unethical way to get to "yes."

I can illustrate this with another memorable movie scene. In *National Lampoon's Christmas Vacation*, Chevy Chase's character receives his Christmas bonus in the form of a jelly-of-the-month club membership. Having already committed the expected money to a new pool, Chase has a mildly hysterical breakdown. His brother-in-law, Randy Quaid, decides the best way to fix this problem is to kidnap the boss and bring him over to the house, bound and gagged with a gold bow on his head. Chase is mortified—but he eventually receives his Christmas bonus. Not a great idea. It worked out in the movies, because everything works out in the movies, but in real life this would have brought horrible consequences down on the family. Good entertainment, bad negotiation strategy.

Putting It into Practice

Recall some of your dreams you've written down in prior chapters. Go through and find one that involves a big obstacle or challenge. Or, maybe you've been asked to do something and you have no clue how to get it done. Either way, start with something that feels fairly impossible to you. Finish the sentence below:

I will not take "no" for an answer about...

Now that it's written up, here's how you develop a plan to get to "yes."

1) Get to common ground.

Like those Harvard guys teach, great negotiations always start with finding common ground. But what does that really mean? Common ground is about focusing on the areas where you already agree. This helps you eliminate potential obstacles and build a place of trust. Part one of the action plan involves writing up all the common ground—focus only on similarities right now.

2) Find a common person.

Relationships are the most important thing in a negotiation, and the quickest way to build common ground. Don't expect others to bend the rules for you, but relationships can bring perspective or balance to negotiation that is very helpful. Most importantly, they reflect trust. When you can work through a mutually trusted third party, it is easier to get to yes. Now, write down all the people who are common to you and the person you're negotiating with.

3) Frame it in a creative way.

My press releases are always fun. Back in my McDonald's days, I announced the opening of the new "PlayPlace" in my restaurant by sending out the little plastic balls from the ball pit. They were gift wrapped in small boxes and on each ball was written, "Want to be a kid again?" For America's Family, I've sent little foam globe balls with a flag sticking out of Colorado

119

that says, "Changing the world starts here." In your situation, what is the most creative way you can package this? What can you do with the "box" you already have? Jot down several ideas.

4) Draw them into your plan.

Everyone loves a good scheme. Did you ever build a tree house or fort with your friends when you were growing up? Who doesn't love that feeling? When I talk to business owners about joining America's Family, I always bring them into my "scheme" to make the world a better place. It's like we're building a tree house together, and soon they're part of the process and giving me ideas. What are some ways that you can draw people into your plan? Write up some of your own schemes.

I want to highlight another hero of mine, Martin Luther King, Jr. He was a guy who never took "no" for an answer, and didn't cut any ethical corners. While leading the civil rights movement of the 1960s, King wore down his opponents through nonviolent civil disobedience. He intended to march on Washington as many times as it took for the country to "get it." King was a great instigator because he wasn't afraid of getting arrested and jailed for his convictions. Through his actions, King rejected segregation. He didn't take "no" for an answer. You don't have to, either. You just need the passionate conviction to pursue your dream by going around, over, past and through anything that gets in your way.

120

Chapter 11

❦

Taking Risks

I am always doing that which I
cannot do, in order that I may
learn how to do it.

Pablo Picasso

I love doughnuts. When I had the opportunity to buy my own Dinky Donut machine, I jumped on it.

I was attending a restaurant convention in Orlando, and in one corner of the exhibit hall was the Dinky Donut demonstration. You could smell it from about 50 feet away, and I followed that smell right to the exhibit. Even now, if there is a convention with a Dinky Donut machine, I will pass up gourmet food, wine, desserts—anything just to get a handful of Dinky Donuts. You've got to imagine a little machine about the size of a small refrigerator. A bucket gently dispenses the doughnut and drops it into a grease trough, a wonderful river of shortening. Then a spatula flips these tiny little doughnuts into the basket, and a second spatula flips them once again into a holding tray under heat lamps. It was exciting to watch, and the smell was just overpowering.

Once the doughnut was cooked, you could pick out your doughnut and either eat it plain or shake it in cinnamon sugar or powdered sugar. I loved everything about it—the river of grease, the little spatulas, and especially the delicious smell of hot, fresh doughnuts. I thought this was the perfect idea for my McDonald's store in the Colorado Springs Citadel Mall.

Halfway through my sixth doughnut (and my third visit to the display), I thought about all the competing smells in the mall's food court. But I had followed my nose to these doughnuts through a crowded exhibit hall with thousands of people in it. I had passed other exhibits with some of the world's finest food. Surely, the smell of these yummy doughnuts would attract customers from across the mall. So, we bought one. Excitedly, we set it up on the counter at the store. I just knew that little kids would come up and press their faces against the plastic shield to watch the doughnuts float down the river. It was so American! A little hot doughnut made to order—what could be better?

Once we got the machine all set up in the store, we prepared the mix according to the instructions, fired up the grease river, and...disaster. The first batch came out looking like French fries. The next batch looked like brains—fried little brains. No matter what we tried, we could not make a Dinky Donut to save our souls. I tried so hard, but I could not recapture that wonderful smell. I couldn't even make one stinkin' edible doughnut from this thing! The machine was great, but something about the production method and the high altitude resulted in the most hideous doughnuts you've ever seen. Hardly anyone was interested in the Dinky Donut machine, because who wants to eat something that looks like a puppy brain? Over the next few months, we got it to work intermittently and got some good traffic, but never was it consistent. Contrary to what I thought, the food court was not filled with the freshly made doughnut aroma. Eventually, I had to take my beloved Dinky Donut machine to my innovation graveyard—where most of my ideas go to die.

There's a place in my warehouse where my seemingly "good" ideas get shelved. Usually, I let them sit there for a few months. We joke about putting on black armbands when we clear out the stuff on the shelves and take it to the dump. The Dinky Donut machine stayed with us for a lot longer. I just couldn't let it go. Every time I saw it, I thought about the wonderful smells and tasty doughnuts from the Orlando Convention Center. "Next time," I'd say, and we'd haul out some other failed projects instead. We go through this about every six months, because far more of my ideas fail than succeed. Over time, you accumulate a lot of failed ideas and have to make room for the next generation. This is a key point of innovation. Don't forget it.

BIGG IDEA: IF YOU'RE AFRAID OF FAILURE, GET OVER IT—EVERYBODY FAILS!

Ron Jensen, a very successful Texas billionaire, told me once that life is not about batting average, but about slugging percentage. Batting average is simply the number of hits divided by the number of at-bats. The greatest players in baseball only hit the ball 30 to 40 percent of the time they step up to the plate. But slugging percentage takes into account the quality of the hit. It divides the total number of *bases* by the number of at-bats. In this calculation, a home run is worth four, while a single is worth only one. Barry Bonds set the all-time slugging percentage record in 2001. He hit 411 bases in 476 at-bats, giving him a slugging percentage of .863.

What does that really tell us about Bonds? Slugging percentage is a measure of overall player production. Bonds swings for the fences—that's his hallmark—and it makes him one hell of a productive player. But swinging for the fences

123

means taking more risks. You have to swing harder, commit sooner and react quicker. There's not much time to think once the 100 mile-per-hour fastball leaves the pitcher's hand. It's go time. In business and in life, you've got to swing for the fences, because that gives you the highest return on your investment.

I always swing for the fences. I swung pretty hard at the Dinky Donut machine. It had "grand slam" written all over it. In fact, my friend Irvin Krueger is making a ton of money on his machine. Now there's a businessman...what a risk-taker! When you're in Times Square, go sit in his McDonald's on 42nd Street and you'll immediately get it. But in my store I could never get the Dinky Donut machine to work. I failed. It wasn't a bad decision; it was just part of the process of trying to make money.

Incidentally, Babe Ruth holds the strikeout record in baseball, and this year Brett Favre will probably break the all-time record for most interceptions in a career. Why? Top achievers take risks that have high rewards. Don't be afraid to try. I've got a million failures—here's another "great" Bigari idea.

There are a lot of rock-climbing walls in Colorado. They have them in malls, outdoor stores and special rock-climbing gyms. I thought a very logical way to make money off of this was to put a first-class, portable rock-climbing wall in the parking lot of one of my stores. Coloradans love burgers, and they love climbing. Why shouldn't they be able to order a Quarter Pounder with cheese and then go scale the wall?

What I didn't consider is that McDonald's hamburgers are inexpensive and fast. Rock climbing is expensive and slow. You need specialized shoes, ropes, hardware, and people who know what they're doing. It's the opposite of the McDonald's

124

food factory model in which an employee makes customized, but mass-produced, food in a matter of minutes. This was an unwise marriage. For the low, low price of $30,000, I invested in a portable, trailer-mounted, top-of-the-line climbing wall. No one used it. But, all was not lost. Because it was portable, we were able to move it down the road to the Garden of the Gods, a national registered landmark in Colorado Springs, where it made $1,200 a day. We served lots of Texas tourists who had nothing but money and time to spend on getting a taste of rock climbing in Colorado. You'd hear them in the park, "Gee, mahmah (mother), wouldn't it be naahce (nice) if we could climb those rocks over there? It's only five daahllars (dollars)." The rock-climbing wall never made it to the graveyard, because I was able to sell it to another guy. It just wasn't right for McDonald's.

My favorite invention was the McDonald's PlayPlace automatic ball washer. The ball pits were filthy from kids playing in them all day long. Everything that kids do got done in my ball pits. Most of the time, they were pretty gross, and sanitation of the ball pits was always a big concern for me. Cleaning them was really expensive and time-consuming. Each pit was about 256 cubic feet—which means a lot of balls to keep clean. At best, you could clean them about once a week. God knows what happened in between. I thought, "We can make this entertaining and engaging, and put the kids to work!" I fashioned a game where kids would throw the balls from the pit into a small target. In the target, they were put into a hopper, washed, sanitized, blown to the ceiling, gently rolled back to earth on a Plexiglas track, and redistributed in the pit. The visual was awesome! It was beautiful. Free labor, the balls were cleaned every day, all day, and it was a game. It worked great, but not enough people adopted this idea, and McDonald's eventually decided to get rid of ball pits altogether. The issues surrounding the ball pit started to create severe liability problems, especially when disgusting and dangerous things started showing up in a few stores. So, gone was the era of the Bigari automatic ball-washer.

You might think I'm crazy. That's really okay by me. People tell me all the time that I'm crazy. But big ideas have paid off for me! Not all of them, but the best ones have made me a lot of money. More importantly, they've given me a platform to speak and to share them. Even when I've failed, every one of my ideas was featured in the local press. That's great promotion and fanfare. My stuff has been in publications ranging from *The Wall Street Journal* to *Rolling Stone*.

As I mentioned earlier, my call center was featured in Thomas Friedman's book *The World is Flat*. You don't get that kind of press by hitting lots of singles. You get it when you become known for cracking home runs in every game. My business success has led to influence in some interesting places. But without all the failures, I would never get to the successes.

Now I find myself in situations where I can use that influence to improve the lives of hard-working, low-wage earners who need help accessing resources they need to build better lives. You never know where swinging for the fences will lead you, which is why it is so fun to wind up that bat and let it rip.

The biggest risk of my career was when I let my daughter, Cali—who was eight years old at the time—write a business plan for a new line of playgrounds for McDonald's. We were on vacation visiting her cousin Greg. During that time, McDonald's share of kid business was dropping, so I thought I'd ask the kids what would make an awesome playground for a store like McDonald's. At this point in Cali's life, basketball was everything to her. She loved it, couldn't get enough of it. But in my stores, we only had the first-generation McDonald's Playlands, which consisted of a ball pit and some plastic tunnels. These were great for little kids, but not for my daughter. So she answered, "Dad, wouldn't it be cool if we could play basketball at McDonald's?"

"You can play basketball at a playground, though," I replied. And we started to banter back and forth about how we could make it like an arcade game that incorporated sports and movement. Eventually, she came up with a game called HotShotz, and she and her cousin pulled out their crayons and pencils to illustrate what the whole game would look like. The end result was a series of timed sports games—basketball, soccer and football. The goal was to get as many points as possible in one minute so that lots of kids could participate. By the time the kids were done, they had eight pages of a crayon-scribbled business plan complete with drawings, rules, instructions for tournaments, and anything else that you'd ever want to know about HotShotz. I thanked them, tossed it in my briefcase, and started to think about how I was going to pitch this to McDonald's. I couldn't just build it myself because I'd probably get in trouble with the corporation. So, I filed it away for another day.

Soon after, I was in a meeting with my new regional manager, Jeff Stratton. Today, he's the corporate executive vice president and chief restaurant officer for McDonald's. He's a great guy with a wonderful sense of humor. This meeting was about Jeff's plan to discuss my acquisition of some additional stores from Larry Kingston. Larry's service to the community was legendary, and I was honored to operate his stores for eight years after he left the business. Like most of the thousands of proprietors out there, Larry continues to live a life of service even today as an executive at Focus on the Family.

I was pushing through some other projects while trying to get McDonald's to put some money on the table so I could buy Larry's stores. Over lunch, I decided, "What the hell, I'm going to show him Cali's plan." So I pulled it out of my briefcase and handed it over to Jeff. I said, "Jeff, would you mind taking a look at this? It's a new playground idea that I think would really work and wanted to get your feedback." Dumbfounded, he took the now slightly wrinkled stack of drawings and smiled awkwardly across the table. His whole face turned white, and I could totally read his mind. He was thinking, "Oh great, I'm trying to get this guy to buy four stores, and he's showing me a business plan in crayon."

He didn't want to be rude or blow the relationship, but, internally, he was rolling his eyes at me. I didn't know what else to do, so I started pitching the plan and walking him through all of Cali's drawings.

By about the sixth page he said, "This is a cool idea! I like it! Do you think you could put it in a PowerPoint presentation or something so we don't get laughed out of the room when we present it?"

"Sure," I said, "no problem." And right there, HotShotz was born.

Over the years, HotShotz evolved through many revisions and evolutions, but it was the first step McDonald's took toward incorporating physical fitness into their play centers. It started with me ripping out a perfectly good $78,000 Playland from my store, and building a $50,000 prototype in its place. I was taking a big risk, but over the past decade, that eight-page set of kids' drawings turned into many more thousands of dollars in profit for my stores. Incidentally, the total value of Cali's idea was worth millions of dollars in new kid business for McDonald's, and that continues to grow today. The next generation PlayPlace and the even-newer R-Gym is built around these types of physical activities. Swing for the fences—you've got nothing to lose.

What Does It Mean to You?

Most people go through their lives without creating or innovating anything. It's not because they don't have the talent. Instead, they are afraid of failure and rejection. Think about it: My 8-year-old daughter took a risk dreaming up a playground idea for her daddy. I was a very successful business operator, so what could I learn from her? She wasn't afraid of sharing her ideas, because we created an environment where it was safe to take risks and fail. She said to me once, "Dad, if you came home and told me that you were going to build a McDonald's on Venus, I'd believe you—and you'd do it, too."

In that safe environment, Cali knew she could dream big. It's one of the most practical applications of this idea that I can think of. You've first got to create an environment where it is safe to dream, risk and fail. Most people laugh at big ideas. "McDonald's on Venus! How stupid is that?" they say. Forget those people. Give me the ones who say, "Okay, well, what do you think the barriers are to getting something like that done?" It's a totally different mindset from what most people have.

As you're thinking about risks you might want to take, I'll only offer you this word of caution. Always ask yourself, "What's the worst thing that could happen?" I learned this from Brent Cameron, and it became a great tool for evaluating whether the timing was right for a particular risky venture. Only you know your risk tolerance, but if the worst-case scenario is unacceptable to you, it's probably not the right time. Put it in your own project file, and come back to it in a few months. You never want to take a risk if the worst-case scenario would literally cripple you financially or otherwise. With HotShotz, I was able to sustain the risk of tearing out a $78,000 playground. It wasn't going to bankrupt me. But if it could have, I wouldn't have done it no matter what the potential reward. I never want to put my ideas ahead of my family, my business success, or the lives of my 500 employees. But in this case, the only person who was going to lose was me.

Putting It Into Practice

I could take a risk and not put an exercise here, but that seems like a cheap way out of coming up with good content. So get that pencil out again.

1) Define the risk you'd like to take.

Sounds easy, but I promise it isn't. Life, by its nature, is full of risks. Narrowing them down into just a few choices could be difficult for you. Think about this in terms of your dreams and passions, and pick one area of your life where you can take a tangible risk. For some people, calling their mother-in-law is a risk—so you don't have to think in terms of $78,000 playgrounds. Put it into your context, and write it out in simple, clear language.

2) Measure your tolerance for risk.

Risk tolerance is really about fear. Certainly, risk comes with the fear of failure, and you've got to determine whether or not you can overcome that fear and move forward. Fear is a cruel master, and I would never advise you to back away from a risk just because you are afraid. But, you have to understand the dynamics of your own risk tolerance so that your mind doesn't play tricks on you when you hit rough patches. By the way, even the most successful innovations in my life were filled with rough patches, some lasting for years!

3) Plan for the worst-case scenario.

This is really hard for the optimists. Finish this question: *The absolute worst thing that could happen to me by taking this risk is...* If any part of your answer involves risking the safety of your family or your ability to continue making money, stop now. There are some risks you do not want to take. Not all risks are equal, and you should take a long, hard look at whether this makes sense for you and your family through the lens of a worst-case scenario.

I know that you can achieve better growth, personally and professionally, if you take more risks. They have to be calculated and smart, and I hope this chapter helps you discover how to find the ones that are right for you. Before closing, I want to give you a little postscript.

You might think that all of my talk about taking risks is common in America's companies today. Unfortunately, this is not the case. In corporate America, "incrementalism" is king. Wall Street rewards companies that make incremental steps forward and don't rock the boat with new big ideas. When did we see the last breakaway company? Google? Google is a company that is really spinning the box. Radical innovation has driven radical growth. Wow! Guess what? Incrementalism gets you incremental growth. How boring. But here's the thinking: Companies don't want 50 percent growth this year because they are afraid of how they'll sustain that growth into the future. They'd rather be up five percent a year for five years instead of 25 percent this year. Do the math on that. You want to be up 25 percent this year and then flat for five years. The time-value of that money is huge! But a company that did that would be punished—severely—by Wall Street. That's a shame. Taking risks is about dynamic, bone-crunching, resource-stretching, radical growth. If that's what you want in your business and in your life, then get your tail in the batter's box and swing for the fences!

Chapter 12

Ready, Fire, Aim

If everything's under control,
you're going too slow.

Mario Andretti

The most sophisticated drive-thru order system in the world operates just outside my office door. During my years at McDonald's, I was continually frustrated by the performance of my drive-thru lanes. They accounted for up to 75 percent of my restaurant revenue, and small mistakes can add up quickly. A four percent mistake rate is not uncommon. On top of that, for it to work right you need a dedicated drive-thru window order-taker. That person simply processes the orders. I started to think, "Why can't I outsource that? What would I need?" I envisioned customers driving up to my McDonald's stores and ordering through the traditional speaker box mounted on the menu board. Except in my dream, they were talking to someone in a call center thousands of miles away. In the call center, an operator would take the order, snap a digital picture of the customer's car, and send both back to the local McDonald's crew, who would prepare the food. As I worked through the system in my head, I knew that a system like this could reduce order time by up to one-third and increase the number of customers served by at least 10 to 15 percent. And I suspected it would slash our error rates and payroll costs. All of these assumptions proved true, and once we implemented the new call center idea, productivity went through the roof.

I don't own the McDonald's stores anymore, but I do advise operators all over the country on the call center and its technology. This type of business didn't exist until I created it with Exit 41 back in 2004. As I related in an earlier chapter, once I got over the software hurdles, the rest fell into place nicely. You have to understand that as a franchisee, it was in my vested self-interest to make the system work more efficiently within the parameters prescribed by McDonald's. That type of self-interest fueled many of my innovations (like the Dinky Donut machine). I realized I would need a call center to support the national rollout of America's Family. After realizing that this call center could be applied to any restaurant ordering model, I decided I needed a building to house it. Specifically, I needed a 20,000 to 30,000 square-foot building to accommodate the expected demand.

For 18 months, I worked with my commercial real estate guys, Sam Cameron and Kevin Butcher, to find a building that would fit our needs. We looked at so many buildings that fit the profile but were expensive, ugly and run-down. I hated all of them. I was so disgusted, I told them to forget it. I would make it work in the little office building I owned. But Sam and Kevin are good friends, and they know how I think. I remember them saying, "Steve, we're going to super-size you. Let's go look at one more building." They were inspired by my call center idea, knew the way my mind worked, and took a risk to show me a building that was about seven times larger than I was looking for! They took me to a 152,000 square-foot building just off Interstate 25 in Colorado Springs. That's about three-and-a-half acres under one roof. On the upside, the owner was a giant British real estate holding company that was desperately trying to get rid of it. Sam had met with the CEO of this firm about a year earlier and remembered him describing this building as "the bane of his existence." It didn't fit their profile and had gone through numerous tenants and various uses.

The most recent tenant had put $7.5 million of improvements into the building, like a diesel back-up generator and the network infrastructure to support 2,500 voice and data lines. By far, it was the most "connected" building that we had looked at. But in this day and age, there is no such thing as a 2,500-seat call center in the US They are a thing of the past, long since outsourced to foreign countries through the wonders of fiber optic cabling. Sam remembered how much this guy hated the building and suspected he'd do just about anything to unload it because the building had been sitting vacant for years. The price was comparable that of a 20,000 to 30,000 square-foot building—a real steal.

But I had to instigate my buddies during this time. I couldn't afford the purchase price on my own. So, as we walked through the building, we began to dream about all of its potential uses. Only a small portion of the building would be devoted to my remote drive-thru call center. With the remainder, we could create a completely new business and make some good money on this investment. Sam and Kevin realized that this was the real estate deal of the century and they wanted in. Incidentally, so did my attorney, my accountant, Matt Favier (my IT guy), and my good friend Joe Johnson. With this group of partners, we bought the building, and set ourselves to the task of figuring out what in the world we'd do with the extra 130,000 square feet we didn't need.

Over the next six months, the purchase progressed through the due diligence phase, and the partners debated and discussed all the potential ideas. In those early days, we seriously considered turning it into:

- an indoor RV parking lot
- a giant indoor storage facility
- a sports and recreation center
- a water park.

With three-and-a-half acres indoors and 15 acres of property, the possibilities were endless. In my career at McDonald's, I had been involved in a lot of innovations related to the kids' playground areas. Now, my connections in the kids' fun industry were coming to bear. Now, I suddenly had a 130,000 square-foot playground to fill, and all the right connections to make that happen.

On the national scene, the fun industry is dominated by giants like Disney and Six Flags. But there are thriving mini-theme parks and activity centers that provide families with a local option for great fun. That was the concept we decided to run with. As partners, our vision was to build a small-market, Disney-like indoor theme park that was fun for kids and inexpensive for parents. And from that vision, Mr. Biggs Family Fun Center was born.

We had a great number of ideas during this time that didn't work out. Our dream of an indoor skateboard park quickly ended once we got the insurance bill. Instead, we put in a dance studio. We closed on the building and began construction that same day. It's what I like to call Bigari Standard Time— that is, everything happens a month sooner than it's supposed to. In Bigari Standard Time, you're always behind. During construction, we had over 500 people—carpenters, artists, designers, food experts—all working toward the goal of making Mr. Biggs a reality. For them, the Mr. Biggs building was just a big blank canvas. Everyone knew that what we were doing would put smiles on kids' faces. Who doesn't love that? The artists and designers really got into the project, incorporating an incredible level of detail. They would get started on something and then add a thousand little things to make it better. They wanted to show their own kids how cool this was.

The months leading up to the opening were a flurry of every kind of activity. We were driven by a very unforgiving deadline. If we missed spring break, we'd lose hundreds of thousands of dollars in potential revenue. This wasn't acceptable to me—and it wasn't acceptable to any of the team either. Through the hard work and dedication of the team, Mr. Biggs opened in just 87 days, in time for spring break in March 2005. In our first week, we did over $250,000 in business.

Inspiration in Motion

This is a clear example of the inspiration, instigation, innovation model. Let's go through it step by step.

First, I had the inspiration to make more money in my drive-thru windows by outsourcing the order-taking to a call center. Once I had a model that worked, I was ready to expand it to a much larger operation, and I needed a building that would accommodate that vision. The real estate guys brought the perfect deal to the table. The expensive infrastructure was exactly what I needed, but the building was seven times larger than what I required. So, we had to figure out how to effectively monetize and build revenue streams around the other 130,000 square feet. The answer to that question was Mr. Biggs Family Fun Center.

137

All this inspiration led to instigation. A project of this magnitude required an army of people, all working together toward a common objective. A guy named Bruce Tuckman, writer and group-dynamic guru, came up with a theory of team dynamics that is called forming, storming, norming and performing. Just as the words indicate, teams form and are initially dependent on a visionary leader. In the storming phase, team members vie for position and authority. This is the most turbulent time in group dynamics, and it is often when people throw in the towel and leave. They literally storm out.

I like to get my teams through the storming phase quickly and into the next level—norming. One way I do this is by creating a "big bad wolf." The big bad wolf is an external problem or enemy that focuses the energy of all the people on the team. For Mr. Biggs, the big bad wolf was the first day of spring break. Everybody knew that we needed to open by then in order to really launch Mr. Biggs. All of the negative energy about the project gets directed at the big bad wolf, not at other team members. This is much healthier for the team and provides a unifying force. It's pretty simple. You're either working toward the goal or you're not. Performance becomes easy to measure. Once teams are properly "normed"—meaning that they begin to function based on a set of written or unwritten "laws" that are shared by all team members—then you can really start making progress. The fourth stage is performing, and it is here that all team members are fully empowered, invested in the outcome and devoting all available resources toward sustaining excellent performance.

The final step, innovation, was actually the easiest for our team. The fully inspired and instigated team began innovating on its own. In the next chapter, I'll tell you about the go-kart track and how it became the best innovation in Mr. Biggs' history. The team knew that it was their job to work with the box they were given. They didn't have the resources of Disney World, just a passionate vision that everyone bought into. So, when you come to Mr. Biggs, you'll see the thousands of little innovations that have transformed it into the premier entertainment venue in the city.

Incidentally, this story also exemplifies other principles of transformative leadership. We took huge risks—no one had ever tried this before. We never took "no" for an answer when we faced a crisis or obstacle. The vision was immense and monumental—and everyone got it! Without collaboration and teamwork, the whole thing would have failed miserably. The team of partners was present every step of the way to help move this endeavor along and score the big wins. We didn't operate this project by remote control from some yacht in the Caribbean. Instead, we were down in the dirt for months with the team, getting this place ready for opening day. My partners are some of my closest friends—but Mr. Biggs never became a frat or a club. Superior performance was demanded of everyone on the team. How else could we have opened in time? Throughout the story, and in my life, these themes continue to crop up. They are all common elements to every one of my successes. But none of this is possible without action first.

BIGG IDEA: READY, FIRE, AIM! EVERY SUCCESS REQUIRES ACTION FIRST.

When we bought the building, it was totally a "ready, fire, aim" experience for us. The deal was so good that we knew we could make money on just about anything we decided to put in there. Of course, we took the time to go through the due diligence process, but we didn't waste a bunch of time coming up with ideas—we just bought the building and kept moving onward toward the goal. Success requires an action-driven life.

Putting It Into Practice

Unfortunately, I can't teach you how to be a more active person. There's a lot about this book that is teachable, but developing an action-oriented mindset is very central to your DNA. You either get it or you don't. Now, I believe that if you have the desire to focus more on taking action, you can do that. But there's no big trick to this; you simply start actually *doing* things instead of just talking about them. The idea of "ready, fire, aim" is to allow yourself to be led more by intuition and gut feelings than by facts, figures, and numbers. Sometimes, you're going to end up with a Dinky Donut machine—or you might just end up with a world-class call center. You never know, and that's the whole point. Without actually acting on your ideas, you'll never know if they're any good.

What I can teach you is how to motivate people to accomplish bigger and better results right where you are today. To do this, we'll focus primarily on how to create a "big bad wolf" or BBW for short. Here's where we start:

1)   What are you trying to accomplish?

Before creating the BBW, decide what you want to accomplish. As a rule, your goals need to be specific, measurable, attainable, and challenging.

- Specific goals are stated in explicit and definite terms.
- Measurable goals are quantifiable using some objective standard.

- Attainable goals are within reach or in some way possible to achieve.
- Challenging goals require stretching beyond what you thought possible.

It is the challenge that draws people together. Lots of goals meet the first three but fail on the fourth. Opening Mr. Biggs on time was a challenging goal for everyone involved. A goal without a challenge is just a task on your to-do list. No one gets excited about to-dos, but people die in the pursuit of worthwhile challenges.

2) Who (or what) is the villain?

Every great story has heroes and villains. Villains give great dramatic tension to otherwise boring situations. Now, you don't want to set up people as villains. That's just mean. So you need to find something else. Look at your situation, and list everything that could become a villain for you. The only rule is that it has to be external. The BBW can't be your accounting department, because that will kill your team. A good BBW is something like a deadline—it's future oriented, out of your control and unforgiving.

3) What barriers can you break down?

You've heard this from me before, but it bears repeating: Your goal as a leader is to break down barriers in the lives of others. In the context of the BBW, your people need to know that you will run through concrete to get the job done. Think about it: If you aren't committed at that level, why should they be? This is the best part of my job. I love it when my employees ask me to break down a barrier because I know that they are getting it. Then they start to manage me! They're saying, "Hey, Steve, I can't get this guy to call me back, and we can't miss our deadline. Would you call his boss and lean on him for me?" Use your influence to break down these kinds of barriers standing in the way.

There's no easy answer here. Many people tell me, "But Steve, this only works because you're involved." I won't deny the truth in that. But that doesn't excuse you from your responsibility as a leader. Great leaders inspire their teams to extraordinary performance. However, you are mistaken to think that great leadership is about personal charisma or financial resources.

I didn't inspire the team. They didn't do this for me. Steve Bigari is just another rich white guy. No, they weren't committed to my financial prosperity: that's just a great byproduct. They received an incremental financial reward for their great performance, but even more, they connected to something bigger than themselves—accomplishing a feat so groundbreaking that they wanted to have their fingerprint on it. You can do this, too, wherever you are and whatever you're working on. Set a goal, find a villain and start ripping down obstacles. You'll find that teams quickly get behind leaders who use these skills.

Chapter 13

~⁀ᴐ

You Can't Put Perfume on a Pig

*"But the Emperor has nothing at all
on!" said a little child.*

From *The Emperor's New Clothes*
Hans Christian Andersen

God delivered Kim Shugart to me about seven years ago. Ovetta Sampson was a reporter for the Colorado Springs *Gazette* who wrote a story about me and America's Family. She had spoken to her neighbor, one she hadn't seen in years, about me and the article. At around the same time, Kim sold his very successful advertising business in California and decided to move here to Colorado Springs. He just so happened to move next door to Ovetta's neighbor. She told her new neighbor, Kim, "You've got to go see this guy Steve Bigari." Then she filled him in about me and America's Family.

So one day this guy, this big burly guy in a sweat suit, showed up at my office. Now, most people knock on my door to get something from me. Money, endorsements, advice—you name it, I've been asked for it. Like I said, this big guy with a raspy voice showed up and said to me, "Mr. Bigari, I don't want anything from you. Just wanted to let you know that I recently moved here from California. I closed my advertising agency. I have plenty of money and don't need a job. I just heard about this great thing you're doing to help poor people, and I want to get involved."

Kim, by far, is the smartest branding guy I have ever met. He created the persona, character and voice for Mr. Biggs. We talk about Biggs like he's a real person around here. Mr. Biggs is a guy who loves his community and stands for timeless values like integrity, honor, and respect. He's a cool-looking guy, tough, always wears sunglasses and has a deep raspy voice (the voice of Kim Shugart). For birthday parties, we have Kim (I mean Mr. Biggs), call up the birthday boy or girl. The heart of who we are as partners is about teaching values to kids. So we created a brand that could actually communicate those values through the fun activities that take place every day. We had solid agreement on the brand, but Kim and I butted heads over another very serious issue—go-karts. Through this, I saw once again how Kim Shugart is a man of fearless integrity.

Forty-seven days before Mr. Biggs was set to open for business, Kim Shugart pulled me into his office and made a startling announcement. "Steve," he said, "I want to put a go-kart track *inside* Mr. Biggs." It was 47 days from our scheduled opening, and he threw this bomb.

"Excuse me?" I said.

"I think we need it," he responded.

"What do we know about a go-kart track?" I asked. Then I got right in his face and said, "Do you realize that we have 47 &$*%@ days until this circus is supposed to open?"

"Yeah," Kim said matter-of-factly. "I think we need it."

You've got to listen to everyone's ideas, even the really bad ones. Around here we call it "kissing frogs." You've got to kiss a lot of frogs before you find a prince. In other words, listen to everyone because you never know when you are going to find the next great idea. Never get so proud that you think that others don't have anything positive to offer. In Kim's case, he actually knew what he was talking about. He's a brilliant guy. He had tons of research on go-kart tracks to back up his idea. There were stacks of binders full of market research on everything go-kart-related. Unlike a lot of people who throw out crazy ideas, Kim had done his homework and was sticking to his guns on this one. He knew without a doubt that if we didn't have a go-kart track, Mr. Biggs wouldn't be world-class family fun.

People have asked me if I went along with the go-kart idea because of my trust in Kim and his marketing genius. That's part of it. But over my career I've made a habit of listening to all the ideas I hear—kissing all the frogs—when making important decisions. If you walked in off the street and said, "Steve, Mr. Biggs needs a go-kart track," I probably would have said, "Let me check into that."

In this case, my relationship with Kim helped us get to a point of decision faster. The idea is always the most important factor, but you also have to consider the relationships at play. Kim and I have years of equity, relationship and trust, and that helps make these wild ideas come to fruition a lot faster. And even in this case, the idea was initially so offensive to me that all I could think to do was punch him in the mouth.

I was in full-on "gotta finish this" mode. How dare he, this Mr. Marketing Guy, come in here and tell me how to change my park? I thought about jumping on him, but he's about twice my size. I wasn't really all that keen about a street fight. I wouldn't suggest you get up in somebody's face and scream at him. It wasn't one of my customary planned instigations. I was emotional. But Kim just kept saying, "Steve, we have to do this. I know. We've gotta do it." Finally, I said, "Okay, let's figure out how to get it done."

145

I'm big on creating signposts that are major indicators to others of what is going on and what is expected. This was *the* watershed moment in the development of Mr. Biggs, so I had to make sure that everyone knew that this was now part of the plan and it would get done by opening day. I was not going to let the opening date slip by even one hour, and I needed a dramatic way to communicate that fact to the rest of the team. As I said in the previous chapter, opening day was the first day of the 2005 spring break, and I knew we'd do at least $250,000 in business during that week alone. If we missed that window, we were pissing away a quarter-of-a-million bucks. There was nothing—not even a go-kart track—that was going to move the opening date. Later that night, when I told the rest of the team that Kim and I were going to build a world-class, go-kart track for our world-class entertainment center, I wanted to make my statement. Now, imagine what a consummate marketing guy's office looks like. The walls are painted bright green. One of the chairs is a bigger-than-life purple hand. He's got goofy toys all over the place. And I walked in with a can of black paint and a brush.

"We're building a go-kart track for Mr. Biggs," I said. Kim and I explained the idea to everyone and answered some of their initial questions. "And we've only got 47 days," I said, and with that I took the brush and painted a big "47" right on the wall of Kim's office. "The go-kart track is a six-month project. We've got 47 days, and it *will* be online and functioning on the day Mr. Biggs opens," I announced. Then we all went to work.

It brought the team together and exponentially influenced the development of the rest of the park. As we began work on the track, the excitement of this project created a scenario in which the sum of the parts became greater than the whole of Mr. Biggs. It infected the entire park, and it elevated the game of every artist, designer, carpenter and craftsman on our job site. Everyone started working faster and with greater levels of creativity. By opening day, the go-kart track was finished, and since that day it has remained the park's number-one attraction. And we owe all that to Kim not being afraid to tell us the truth.

In the process of bringing the go-kart track to life, we had to navigate six months' worth of hurdles in less than seven weeks. We decided to go with electric go-karts, since we were catering to little kids and families. But the first significant hurdle was how to design the track in a room that was a bit too small for a go-kart track. We called it the Night Rider Speedway. Next door to the Speedway is the laser tag arena, otherwise known as the SS Vistromo. We continued the laser tag theme into the Night Rider Speedway with the storyline that an alien ship irradiated the area throughout the go-kart track. That's why there are giant rats, ants the size of dogs, burned-out buildings, and the menacing aliens themselves. Initially, we wanted to mount laser cannons on the front of all the go-karts so kids could shoot the radioactive monsters and accumulate points. We also realized that we'd need a twisty track full of curves and turns. An oval track seemed dull, not terribly exciting. But a twisty track puts more wear on the vehicles, so we had to come up with a system of rotating the cars in and out of service, and reversing the track occasionally so that we distributed the wear evenly on the kart.

These three challenges—the configuration of the track, the laser guns, and creating the theme of the area—were the top three challenges for our team. We went through three prototype laser guns in the first year before abandoning the idea: a 50-

147

caliber cannon, a small handgun, and a traditional laser tag gun. They ended up in the innovation graveyard and, eventually, the dump. No one cared about the guns. The kids just loved the experience of driving the cars through the burned-out, alien-infested, cityscape that we built.

What Does It Mean to You?

Organizations that are run by fear are never great. Excellent organizations are led by people who surround themselves with brilliant people, like Kim Shugart. But more than building a good team, they create an environment where it is safe to challenge the leader, get in his face and disagree with his perception of reality. It is legendary how Kim and I butt heads around here—so much so that it makes me crazy! But it tells everyone that it's okay to butt heads with me, that I will always listen to you—even if I don't agree with you. If I don't, I'm going to tell you exactly why. I tell people, "If you can fix that and bring it back to me, we'll take it forward, and I'll commit to making it a success." Kim and I started that meeting chest-to-chest with my finger in his face. But when we left, we were shoulder-to-shoulder—ready to build that attraction at all costs. I embraced it as if it were my own idea, and we ran with it. I could've said, "Hey, guys, look at Kim's dumb-ass idea to build a go-kart track. Isn't that the craziest thing you've ever heard?" Nope, that's not my style. I agreed with Kim, and I gave him 100 percent of my resources to make it happen. No questions asked. Nobody questioned how committed I was to the go-kart track idea because I made it my own and pulled out the stops to make it a success.

I have a low tolerance for dissent once the team has made a decision. I'm talking about when a team gets together and makes a decision corporately, and then someone comes to me privately and says, "Hey, Steve, I don't think this will work." People like this do not get it, and they present me with one option: Get rid of them. The time for dissent and questions is when the decision is being made. Bring on the objections during the decision-making process. Tell me all the worst-case scenarios. But once the team commits, I expect that everyone is 100 percent on-board. If people can't do that, then it's time to show them the door because they have integrity problems. Sounds a little cutthroat, but nothing will kill a team faster than an armchair quarterback. Bottom line: It's an integrity issue. You can't sit in a room and agree with the team and then push a contrary agenda after the fact. I don't listen to armchair quarterbacks—I fire them.

When we made the decision, we all agreed that we could only do an oval track. But down the road we realized that would be a bore. So the team got together, and we chose a different direction. Obstacles and challenges will often force you to revise or edit your original decisions. It's one of the things you need to expect when you have a "ready, fire, aim" approach to life. But you've got to have people around you who will tell you the truth—even when it's hard to hear.

I didn't want to hear that an oval track wasn't right. Financially, it was exactly the way to go. Cars run on an oval track have fewer maintenance and repair issues. So what? Oval tracks are like a hamster wheel. Who wants to go in a circle again and again? So the team came up with a plan to overcome the obstacles so we could make the go-kart track with curves and twists, so it would be a lot more fun. That design ups the anticipation value, and our financial models showed us that the investment in a more expensive go-kart track would pay off in the long run.

Again we come back to removing barriers to success. When people tell me, "Steve, that can't be done in 47 days," I always turn the question around and say, "Well, what would it take and what would you need to get it done in 47 days?" You see, in Bigari Standard Time, everything is possible. By turning the objection into an opportunity, I'm pulling out of my team some of the potential obstacles. Together, we prioritize them and agree on the most important.

I tell my kids, "If I could fill the minivan with candy, I would, but I can't." You see, we all want what we can't have. Unlimited candy—not realistic or good. It's not a world of unlimited resources, so we need to determine what the most important priorities are and let everything else go. Once the team agrees on the priorities, I can remove the barriers and get out of the way.

In a nutshell, this is about casting a big vision, setting the team in place, removing the obstacles to success, and then getting out of the way. When that happens in Bigari Standard Time, you're even better off. You get the best ideas, and they are accomplished in a time and fashion that no one can believe. It becomes incredibly valuable to the psyche of the team. They begin to believe they can do almost anything. This confidence is one of the hallmarks of a world class team.

BIGG IDEA: YOU CAN'T PUT PERFUME ON A PIG. (WELL, YOU CAN, BUT IT'S STILL A PIG.)

Putting It Into Practice

Think about *The Emperor's New Clothes*. Everyone is afraid to tell the emperor that he's parading around in his underwear. But the little kid can't help himself. That's really the heart of integrity: seeing the world as it is and describing it in truth and sincerity. If you want to be a person of great integrity, it takes a tremendous amount of effort and daily discipline. Fortunately, the concepts are simple, and most of them you learned as a child.

1) Practice the Golden Rule.

Treat others in the same way that you'd like to be treated. That's really revolutionary today. Every time I see someone get cut off on the road I wonder if that's how that driver expects to be treated. Probably not. (He's probably the same guy screaming at you when you won't let him merge into traffic.) One of the best ways to cultivate integrity is to treat people the way you would want others to treat you.

Now, that doesn't mean that you give people the same things that you like. Just because you like Johnnie Walker Blue Label scotch doesn't mean that everyone else will. No, practicing the Golden Rule means studying people around you and determining what delights them, and then doing it for them. It's about self-denial and paying attention—then doing things the way others like to have them done. The best way to practice this is to start with someone who is really difficult, someone you really dislike. Study this person's activities for about a week. Observe what he or she does, how this person acts, works, treats others, and makes decisions. Then think about ways to incorporate that data into your relationship with this person.

151

2) Always tell the truth.

Do it—even if it hurts! Every day we are tempted to tell little falsehoods, white lies. Sometimes we don't even know we are doing it. People of integrity, like Kim Shugart, always tell the truth. It's hard to tell the truth to people who don't want to hear it, but it's your job.

There's a difference between truth-telling and brutal honesty. Telling the truth is something you should practice every day. Brutal honesty should be reserved for times when only blunt-force trauma can get the job done. I'm brutally honest. If something looks stupid, I usually say, "That looks stupid." I apologize and everything's okay. But you should develop some tact. This week, I want you to pick a hard truth. Maybe your best friend has body odor or your assistant has bad breath. Whatever it is, find it, write up a tactful and other-centered way to convey the message, and then sit down and have the conversation. By packaging your truths in the spirit of the Golden Rule, you can convey them with grace—rather than with a Bigari sledgehammer.

These elements of integrity are foundational. This short chapter is not a full treatment of the subject, but what I look for in great employees is the ability to treat others well and the ability to tell the truth. Those two things will never betray you. If all else fails, think like a kid. They are the most honest humans on the planet. You might try something I do with my kids called "cut and choose." When the kids are fighting over, for example, a piece of cake, I ask one of them to cut it in half.

Then I ask the other child to choose which piece he wants. After a while, the kids get it, and they want to cut the pieces according to the Golden Rule. It's fun to watch them cut it as evenly as possible. Hopefully through this lesson, Brenda and I are teaching them a little something about integrity and truth. Feel free to steal that one. I did.

Chapter 14

Transforming the World You Live In

Find something you're passionate about and
keep tremendously interested in it.

Julia Child

I said it in the beginning of the book—and it bears repeating! What matters most is what you do with the box you got—right where you are. What is that box? It's yours to define! And it can be anything that motivates you, quickens your heart, or gives you a sense of anticipation. Once you see the vision, maybe a personal quest or a dream for your professional life, then you can begin taking steps to achieve it. You accomplish it by first understanding *and living* the idea that each one of us has influence. You are a leader.

BIGG IDEA: WE ARE ALL LEADERS.

When we started the book, I shared with you that leadership is not about formulas and recipes. It's all about combining the right ingredients and, fueled by passion, using them in unique ways to achieve your vision. Let's review the ingredients:

Inspiration

BIGG IDEA: ADOPT THE
ATTITUDE OF "WHY NOT?"

Inspiration begins with the simple question, "Why not?" Why not credit-card purchases for a fast-food joint...a remote call center to serve people in the drive-thru line...47 stinkin' days to build a twisty go-kart track? Beyond asking the question, it's adopting a new perspective for seeing the world you live in.

Instigation

BIGG IDEA: USE THOUGHTFUL INSTIGATION TO
MAKE YOUR POINT.

Instigation helps move an idea from concept to reality, like with the drive-thru window problems. I had to move the crew from the concept of better performance to the reality of better performance. My vehicle: a flying packet of BBQ sauce. Instigations come in all shapes and sizes. The point is to use your influence to show others the right course of action in a thoughtful, memorable and unconventional way—it's a way to infect them with your vision.

Innovation

BIGG IDEA: IT'S WHAT YOU DO
WITH THE BOX YOU GOT!

Innovating really gets my heart pumping. Yet, it's so simple. Most of my great ideas are the combination of two or

156

more existing products or services. Putting them together in new ways leads to something entirely new. Innovation: Anyone can do it, but it requires the right combination of ingredients to bring it to life.

Vision

BIGG IDEA: VISION ALWAYS ATTRACTS TALENT.

Vision is foundational in all of the examples I've given you in this book. Whether on the football field, in the Army, at McDonald's, Mr. Biggs or America's Family, vision is a key ingredient to leadership. In fact, I don't think leaders can exert effective influence unless they have a vision that is big, bold and extremely contagious. Let's say your vision is baking a chocolate cake. Then your job is to get everyone on your team to smell it baking, visualize licking the frosting from the spoon, and realize the great pleasure in taking a bite before the first egg ever cracks over the side of the bowl.

Presence

BIGG IDEA: YOU MUST BE PRESENT TO WIN

And your presence can't be limited to showing up. That's a part of it, but you must be actively present, your mind as well as your body. It's truly one of the only ways you can effectively incorporate the other ingredients listed in this book. You can't instigate or remove barriers if you aren't around. Who sets a vision from a thousand miles away? Great leaders are accessible. Like Favre in that unforgettable December 22,

2003, game—when you are present, when every part of you is engaged, you can, and will, exert influence and motivate others to win.

Team

BIGG IDEA: ALWAYS CONSIDER THE QUESTION, "WHAT'S IN IT FOR ME?"

It sounds like a strange question when talking about team—but in reality, self-interest is a prime motivator. My concept of team was first formed by watching the Green Bay Packers of the 1960s. There's a reason these guys are the gold standard of teamwork in the NFL. They are absolutely legendary—not for their talent, but for their interaction as a unit. And you can bet each one is invested in his personal interest—whether that's achieving a personal best, breaking records or winning games. And you can rarely accomplish anything worthwhile on your own. A leader's job is to assemble a group of people who are smarter and more technically skilled than he is himself. Then set them free to accomplish great things.

Service

BIGG IDEA: YOU WILL NEVER HAVE ALL YOUR NEEDS COMPLETELY MET. MEET THE NEEDS OF OTHERS ANYWAY.

This is one of the great countercultural ideas of our time, especially when it comes to business dealings. Yet the best expression of leadership comes through serving the people in your life—your employees, friends and family. I serve my team by listening to new ideas and helping remove barriers and obstacles to success. Find ways to serve, reward and motivate your team. It will only mean greater success.

Commitment

BIGG IDEA: LIFE IS NOT A FRAT. YOU'RE EITHER 100 PERCENT IN OR 100 ERCENT OUT.

As Maj. Weller so powerfully communicated: If any part of you is reserved, then you're not truly committed. Real commitment means being honest with yourself and those around you. Leaders with integrity, like Maj. Weller, are effective because honesty engenders trust and respect. Too many businesspeople today think so much of appearance, from personal to overall corporate performance, that they skew (or outright distort) the truth in order to look better in the short-term. It never pays off in the long run. Your relationships, personal or business, are based on performance—not how great you look in the limelight, but how trustworthy you are in the trenches.

Persistence

BIGG IDEA: YOU CAN'T TAKE "NO" FOR AN ANSWER.

Find a way. Remember the silver punchbowl? The Skull wasn't taking "no" for an answer, so I had to get creative in meeting his request. There's always a path that will get you to "yes." Again, this concept dovetails nicely with teamwork, performance, and presence. Those other ingredients help you marshal the resources to get beyond "no" and toward "yes."

Risk

BIGG IDEA: IF YOU'RE AFRAID OF FAILURE, GET OVER IT—EVERYBODY FAILS!

Take risks! Adding the ingredient of risk to your leadership requires mastery over fear. Remember my advice about swinging for the fences? Risk takes guts—and getting up off your duff even when you don't have all the pieces of the puzzle in front of you. Sometimes it pays off; other times you strike out. My Dinky Donut machine endeavor didn't turn out so successfully—but that was a frog I couldn't resist! Many of my frogs have turned into big princes.

Action

BIGG IDEA: READY, FIRE, AIM! EVERY SUCCESS REQUIRES ACTION FIRST.

Leaders resist inertia through movement and action. Creating Mr. Biggs Family Fun Center in time for spring break was a huge undertaking that took a great deal of detail and planning. But the key to carrying it out was a unilateral commitment to action—we pulled the trigger and shot ahead. Leadership without action and motivating your team to move forward is impossible. You've got to commit—through fear, risk and insane timelines—to achieving your vision.

160

Integrity

BIGG IDEA: YOU CAN'T PUT PERFUME ON A PIG. (WELL, YOU CAN, BUT IT'S STILL A PIG.)

My friend and coworker Kim Shugart is a man of integrity, so when he came to me with a seemingly impossible idea (once I got over the initial shock), I cleared the path to make the go-kart track a reality. It's not easy to call things as you see them—you risk being ridiculed, laughed at, or—as in Kim's case—having someone square off with you. Build trust equity with the people in your life based on character, integrity, and reliability. Like the little child in "The Emperor's New Clothes," don't be afraid to call 'em as you see 'em.

Taking the First Step

Most great leaders use stories to teach key principles. Without making a claim to greatness, I've tried to show you the most effective leadership principles by telling stories about my experiments with the raw ingredients. Through these stories, I've attempted not only to impart information, but also to set it in the proper context. Everything here is cobbled together out of the stuff of Steve Bigari. I hope they have torn down much of the conventional wisdom of our time.

I hope I have stirred up a little something in you—a little inner turmoil—that will help get you started on your own journey. Take these stories at face value from a person like you who combined the ingredients of leadership and has experienced great success. I think you can do that, too. And it all comes full circle to looking deep inside yourself, getting in touch with your passions and allowing them to transform you and the people around you as they catch your vision.

As you consider what you want to do next, I want to leave you with one final word of advice: Don't wait another minute. Start big, start small, but get going. Taking action is the only way to achieve transformational leadership. I can't promise you'll become a millionaire, but I can guarantee you a lifetime's worth of fulfillment and great stories along the way. Good luck!

References

This is attributed to Socrates on Wikiquote and others
Wikiquote. (2006). Socrates – Wikiquote. Retreived October
13, 2006, from http://en.wikiquote.org/wiki/Socrates (5)

Visa. (2006). Visa Advertising. Retrieved October 17, 2006
from, http://usa.visa.com/about_visa/press_resources/com-
pany_profile/visa_brand.html?it=il|/personal/visa_brings_
you/advertising/index.html|Get%20the%20Details%26nbsp
%3B (19)

Wikipedia. (2006). Paul McCartney -Wikipedia. Retrieved
October 17, 2006 from http://en.wikipedia.org/wiki/Paul_
McCartney#Yesterday (23)

John F. Kennedy. (May 25, 1961). "Urgent National Needs" A
speech before a joint session of Congress. (23)

Ronald Reagan. (January 17, 1983). "National Security Decision Directive Number 75" a memo by President Reagan.

William Shakespeare (1992). Hamlet. New York: Washington
Square Press (29)

Democracy Now. (September 5, 2005). Kanye West: "Bush
doesn't care about black people." Retrieved October
17, 2006 from http://www.democracynow.org/article.
pl?sid=05/09/05/1453244 (30)

Govleaders.org (2006). "Promoting Better Leadership and Management in the Public Service." Retrieved October 17, 2006 from http://www.govleaders.org/quotes5.htm (40)

John F. Kennedy. (May 25, 1961). "Urgent National Needs" A speech before a joint session of Congress. (57)

Steven R. Covey. (1989). Seven Habits of Highly Effective People. New York: Simon and Schuster.

Search on October 18, 2006 at www.Google.com. (59)

"Triumph of the Nerds," Transcript. http://www.pbs.org/nerds/part1.html (61)

Deborah J. Baker. (2003). Ward's Business Directory of US Private and Public Companies, 46th Edition. Farmington Hills, MI: Thomson Learning Inc. (63)

Collins Quotation Finder. (1999) Glasgow: Harper Collins. (65)

"Triumph of the Nerds," Transcript. http://www.pbs.org/nerds/part1.html (68)

Brainy Quote. (2006). Brett Favre Quotes. Retrieved October 17, 2006, from http://www.brainyquote.com/quotes/quotes/b/brettfavre179461.html. (68)

Brett Favre, Bonita Favre, Chris Havel. (2004). Favre: For the Record. New York: Rugged land, LLC. (72)

Section 2. (Aug. 21, 1997) New York Times 126:11 (73)

David Packard. (1996). The HP Way: How Bill Hewelett and I Built Our Company. New York: Harper Collins. (73)

Suzy Welch, (September 2006). " 10-10-10" O The Oprah Magazine, Hearst Communications, Inc. (75)

Andrew Carnegie http://chatna.com/author/carnegieandrew. htm (81)

Tom Waldron, Brandon Roberts and Andrew Reamer with assistance from Sara Rab and Steve Ressler. (October 2004). "Working Hard, Falling Short." Working Poor Families Project. (81)

Eric Schlosser. (1998). Fast Food Nation. New York: Houghton Mifflin. (82)

Thomas L. Friedman. (2005). The World Is Flat: a brief history of the twenty-first century. New York: Farrar, Straus and Giroux. (87)

Dr. Kent Keith. (1968). The Paradoxical Commandments. Published by Dr. Kent Keith. (95)

"Bless the Broken Road," Rascall Flatts, Feels Like Today, Lyric Street Records, 2004. (97)

www.quotationbook.com (108)

Robert Zemeckis. (1994). Forrest Gump. Paramount Pictures. (126)

Peter Farrely. (1994). Dumb and Dumber. Motion Picture Corporation of America, New Line Cinema. (127)

Hans Christian Andersen, adapted and illustrated by Eve Thalet and translated by Rosemary Lanning. (2000). The Emperor's New Clothes. New York: North South Books (154)